The *Titanic*'s stern lifted up, up, up until the ship pointed straight toward the stars like some giant's black accusing finger.

Vibrations convulsed through Alfreda's arms as every movable object inside the ship—from china teacup to grand piano—broke loose, hurled, and slammed down through the hull. Everywhere she glanced she saw people clinging together in clusters and bunches like swarming bees. *If only we had wings.*

Wooden deck chairs and barrels flew past her. Then bodies with legs and arms waving. *Splash! Splash!* She had only seconds. She knew it. With all her strength, she pushed herself away from the ship, held her nose, and leaped into the deadly cold water.

Books by Laurie Lawlor

The Worm Club
How to Survive Third Grade
Addie Across the Prairie
Addie's Long Summer
Addie's Dakota Winter
George on His Own
Gold in the Hills
Little Women *(movie tie-in)*

Heartland series
Heartland: Come Away with Me
Heartland: Take to the Sky
Heartland: Luck Follows Me

American Sisters series
West Along the Wagon Road 1852
A *Titanic* Journey Across the Sea 1912
Voyage to a Free Land 1630
Adventure on the Wilderness Road 1775
Crossing the Colorado Rockies 1864
Down the Río Grande 1829
Horseback on the Boston Post Road 1704

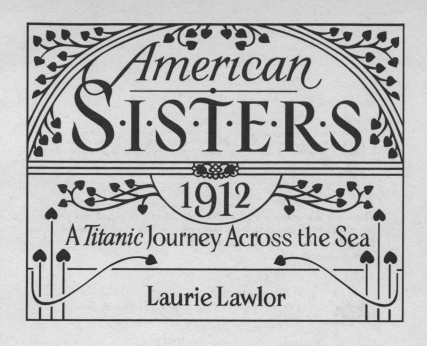

American S·I·S·T·E·R·S

1912

A *Titanic* Journey Across the Sea

Laurie Lawlor

A MINSTREL® BOOK

Published by POCKET BOOKS
New York   London   Toronto   Sydney   Singapore

A Minstrel Book published by
POCKET BOOKS, a division of Simon & Schuster, Inc.
1230 Avenue of the Americas, New York, NY 10020

Copyright © 1998 by Laurie Lawlor

Originally published in hardcover in 1998 by Minstrel Books

ISBN: 0-671-77559-6

First Minstrel Books paperback printing November 2000

10 9 8 7 6 5 4 3 2 1

A MINSTREL BOOK and colophon are registered trademarks of Simon & Schuster, Inc.

Cover illustration by Nanette Biers

Printed in the U.S.A.

For my greatgrandparents
Anna Louisa Johannesdotter
and Johannes Nilsson,
who sailed to America in 1881

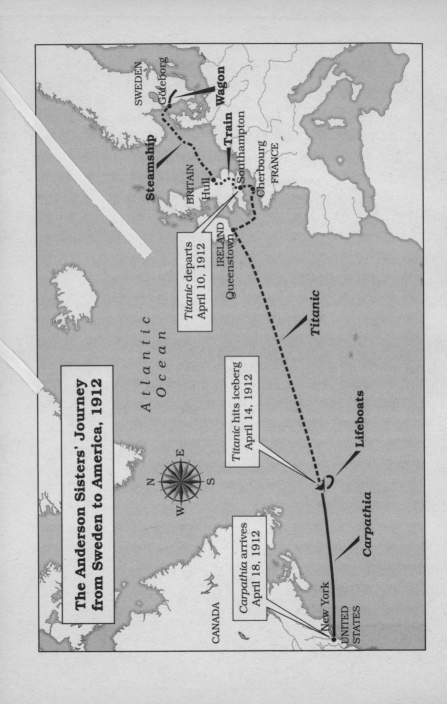

The Anderson Sisters' Journey from Sweden to America, 1912

Atlantic Ocean

N
E
W
S

SWEDEN

Göteborg

Wagon

Train

Steamship

Southampton

Cherbourg

FRANCE

BRITAIN

Hull

*Titanic departs
April 10, 1912*

IRELAND

Queenstown

Titanic

*Titanic hits iceberg
April 14, 1912*

Lifeboats

Carpathia

*Carpathia arrives
April 18, 1912*

CANADA

New York

UNITED
STATES

Chapter 1

Alfreda Anderson had been away from home so long, she felt like a stranger. The wagon lurched down the muddy road, bumping over rocks and ruts and splashing through puddles of spring rain. *What if I'm too late?*

She scanned the empty, fallow fields. Beyond stood a sea of stumps. Once upon a time she recalled rye rippling and whispering in the wind. She recalled a cool, dark forest where she burned her legs on stinging nettles while gathering mushrooms. Nothing looked familiar now. An uneasy feeling coiled in the bottom of her stomach like a snake hiding in the crannies of a stone fence.

The wagon creaked up a hill, past a clump of

juniper that half-hid a broken, weathered gate. Not far away she glimpsed a pile of stones, a caved-in roof, and empty, staring windows that reminded her of vacant eyes. "Where are the Nilssons?" she called to the wagon driver, who fumbled with his box of snuff.

"Corporation bought their place, so they emigrated," he replied. "No one stays in Sweden anymore. They go to *Amerika.*"

Amerika. Alfreda sighed. Even the word was beautiful and full of promise. *A-mer-i-ka.*

A cuckoo sang from an alder. Soon she'd see her grandparents' cottage, where everyone would be waiting for her. She sat up very straight, very tall, gathered her worn wool shawl around her sturdy shoulders, and hoped she looked grown up. She was sixteen years old. The last time she'd been home, she was thirteen and had just finished her confirmation with honors. Would anyone remember how well she read aloud that day? So many high hopes for her—the finest scholar in the parish. Everyone said she'd go on to the *seminaria* to study, then perhaps she'd get a job as a teacher. . . .

Alfreda's shoulders sagged. *So much big talk!*

There was no money for more schooling, Mama had told her. For the past three years Alfreda had worked for her keep with her uncle, the tailor in Alna. She rose at dawn to cook, milk the cows, and clean the house. Not once did her stingy aunt offer to pay her. Not once did anyone talk to her or treat her like anything more than an ignorant hired servant who slept in the kitchen corner. Only when Mama's letter arrived was she finally allowed to return to Värmland for a visit.

"Your brother is dying. Come home."

Alfreda craned her neck when she saw chimney smoke floating overhead. The road zigzagged through a stand of apple trees. Wind shook delicate white apple blossoms down on her. The sweet, damp petals clung to her hair like snow and made her feel strangely happy. Surely Mama had been wrong. Little Karl would get better. In this season of so much promise, so much sunlight, he would grow strong.

When Alfreda had left home, her thin, big-eyed brother with the wispy pale hair had just turned four. He had always coughed, ever since he was a baby. Sometimes he would turn nearly blue trying to breathe. And he cried too much. He was spoiled, that much was certain. Mama never scolded him when he dipped his curious, dirty fingers into the bread bowl.

No matter how hard Alfreda tried, she could

not vividly recall Karl's face. She squeezed her eyes shut, struggling to imagine the shape of his nose, his forehead, his mouth. Anything. *Of course, won't he look different now?* He was born in 1905. Seven years earlier. The same year they moved in with her grandparents. The same year Papa left.

Suddenly the wagon stopped.

Alfreda flew forward, eyes open. Yes, this was her grandparents' cottage. She was certain. There were the squared pine log walls and the roof shingled with layers of birch bark. She spied the worn stone steps and the arched garden trellis—exactly as she had left them. But what were these many strangers' wagons and carriages doing here? Whose horses were these that stood impatiently pawing the ground?

Something is wrong.

She jumped from the wagon and ran to the cottage door, not even stopping to answer when the wagon driver called, "What about your trunk?"

She pushed the door open. The small cottage was hot, stuffy, and crowded with neighbors. They turned like a herd of sheep and looked at her with pitying expressions.

"Poor, poor thing!" bleated ancient Olga. For

good measure, she spit—a sure means to keep the powers of darkness at a distance.

"Such a lovely burial at the churchyard, too," murmured Helda, the blacksmith's widow.

"That new shirt with the lace collar," Olga added. "So beautiful."

Alfreda stumbled past the women. Beside the fireplace sat Mama in a black kerchief pulled around her face so that it covered her sunken cheeks. Long ago people called her the village beauty. Now her skin was as tough as a winter apple and white streaked her yellow hair. Her back was bent from too many hours hunched over the sewing machine. She did not embrace Alfreda. She only looked up with sad, accusing eyes and said, "He's gone."

Alfreda did not know what to do, what to think. She watched the villagers dipping chunks of bread into mugs of coffee and making loud sucking noises. Someone had baked a sweet cake with a big black sugar cross in the middle. The table groaned with platters of meatballs and stewed peas and boiled potatoes and sweet cheese—more food than Alfreda had seen in more than a year. But she did not feel hungry. She did not feel anything.

She stared at Grandfather's army comrades,

who sipped *brännvin*, a strong mourning drink. They wiped their gray mustaches with the backs of their hands and nodded solemnly when they noticed her. She did not hear them when they uttered clumsy condolences.

Too late.

Someone grabbed her by the elbow and pulled her. Tiny, deaf Grandmother thrust into Alfreda's hands two sweetmeats wrapped in black paper on which had been pasted paper angels with white wings. Grandmother held fast to Alfreda and steered her through the crowd to Grandfather. He sat on a low stool beside Old Klinta-Kitta, who had cured many people of bone fever, dropsy, and blood infection. *Why couldn't she save Karl?*

"Alfreda!" Grandfather said, struggling to his feet. He hugged her so hard she could not breathe. "Our poor little one's gone to Jesus. His cough . . . his cough—" He bit his lip, unable to go on.

"God rest his soul," piped up Old Klinta-Kitta. She gulped her *brännvin*. "Your mother owes everyone in town trying to find a cure. When he was too far gone for any of my herbs to work, she bought every elixir, every quack medicine—"

"Hush now, Klinta-Kitta," Grandfather murmured. "He was her only son."

Noisy Old Klinta-Kitta paid no attention to his

warning. "An America-widow should be more careful with her money. A husband gone seven years. That's a very long time. He might never come back."

"Enough now, Klinta-Kitta!" Grandfather said, louder this time. He turned and smiled at Alfreda, but his mouth quickly collapsed at the corners. "Where is your little sister? I am sure she would like to see you. We shall find her. Soon our guests will be leaving. Erna must say goodbye."

Alfreda nodded. She felt dazed and numb, as if she were helplessly watching a bad dream unfolding. *When will I wake up?* She shuffled behind Grandfather, past Mama's gleaming sewing machine, which had been covered with a black cloth. In her hand she still clutched the little paper with the angels and the uneaten sweetmeats. *Erna.* She had completely forgotten about her seven-year-old sister. No. Now she was ten. Erna was ten years old. *Perhaps she will not remember me, either.*

As she made her way past the mourners, Alfreda put one foot in front of the other and prayed that she would not be stopped by a neighbor and have to talk and pretend to be sad. *What is wrong with me?*

"Erna has always been such a good and loving

child." Mama's voice drifted past. "So obedient. Never a disappointment. Nothing like Alfreda . . ."

Nothing like Alfreda. Alfreda stumbled toward the door. Her wooden shoes seemed to be as heavy as iron. She couldn't breathe. *Faster! Get out!*

"But have you heard my America-letter? Why, of course not. You're just home from your aunt and uncle's," Olaf the shoemaker said. He held on to Alfreda's sleeve. Before Alfreda could wriggle away and follow Grandfather out the door, Olaf waved a piece of expensive America-paper in her face. "Listen to this. It's from my sister in Brooklyn, America."

Alfreda had to listen. She had no choice. The reading of an America-letter was as important as the reading of a sermon by the parish clergyman. Whenever a letter came, everyone in the village heard the words at least twice. Reading an America-letter was a chance to share one's relative's good fortune.

Olaf cleared his throat importantly and read aloud:

❧

"*Dearest Brother:*
    Whew! So hot it is, the sweat runs off me as I write. You may be sure it is warm

enough so we don't have to blow into our
hands any longer. Now we have to blow *on*
them instead. . . . I ate strawberries on Sunday, while out with an American family.
They live in the same house as we do, so we
are together a lot. He is a mate on a boat
that goes on the river; I have supper almost
every Sunday evening with them, for we
play dominoes with them, and so they ask us
to stay for supper. I believe no other nation
is as hospitable as the Americans, but they
will not stand any ceremony. They will invite
you just once and if you stand on ceremony,
then you have to take the consequences. . . ."

Alfreda pushed past bragging Olaf. She had to
get air. She had to escape. While the rest of the
guests argued about whether the strawberries in
Brooklyn could be as sweet as the strawberries
in Sweden, Alfreda rejoined her grandfather. He
waited patiently outside the cottage beside an old
sway-backed horse.

"Your sister's in the barn," Grandfather said
slowly. He kept stroking the horse as if by doing
so he would not have to look at her directly.
"She's grieving pretty badly."

Alfreda's cheeks burned. She clenched her teeth. *Nobody cares how I feel.*

"Be especially kind to Erna, will you?" Grandfather said. He turned to go back inside the cottage. "Tell her she must return to Boppa and say goodbye to our guests."

"Yes, Grandfather," Alfreda said, refusing to call him the babyish nickname her sister always used. *Erna. "So obedient. Such a good and loving child. Never a disappointment."* Suddenly Alfreda had the irresistible urge to punch the sister she had not seen in three years. Then she'd scream at Mama and their guests, "Leave me alone!"

She did none of those things. Instead she trudged to the cool, dark barn that smelled of sweet dried grass and leather harness and the sweat of horses and cows. Flies buzzed. Mourning doves cooed. In the barn no one chattered about lace-collar burial clothes. No one boasted about strawberries. Life was peaceful.

Erna heard her sister's wooden shoes *clunk-clunka-clunk* across the wooden floor. Erna hid behind a bale of hay and watched her older sister carefully. *She's not the way I remember.* Alfreda's ash-blond hair, which hung in a spindly braid down her back, looked darker. Her face was narrower, more serious. Her blue eyes darted this way and that, trying to find Erna.

Erna smiled. She was good at hiding. She and her cousin Anna loved to wander in the forest and build fern-and-moss huts. They dressed in magic outfits made with flowers and leaves. They explored the woods and clambered among the ruins of an ancient castle surrounded by a moat. Sometimes they pretended to be invisible—the way she was doing right now.

Carefully Erna shifted the small bowl of porridge and the sweet cake into her other hand. This was her offering for the *tomte*. She peered into the darkness of the barn's highest rafters. Up there in the shadowy corners, Boppa said, the *tomte* might be watching her at this very moment. Although a *tomte* stood no taller than her waist, he was in fact a very old man. The *tomte* was a wise and secretive fellow who came out only at night. She had only caught glimpses of him wearing his home-woven gray wool jacket, knee breeches, wooden shoes, and red nightcap. "Nothing defiled, nothing wasted. That's what keeps the *tomte* coming back to our farm," Boppa had told her. As long as they took care of the *tomte*, the *tomte* would take care of them.

Erna placed the bowl on the wooden floor. The

sudden *thud* made Alfreda call out fearfully, "Who's there?"

Erna held her breath. She didn't want to speak to this stranger, her sister. Not now. She crouched lower. But she was too late.

"Get up, you little scamp," Alfreda announced. Her hands were on her hips. She frowned. "What are you doing wasting good food?"

"It's for the *tomte*," Erna mumbled. She stood up slowly. Her sister was much taller than she remembered.

"What foolishness is this?" Alfreda sputtered. She stared hard at her younger sister. *Still so small and skinny. Does no one feed her?* "You are too old to believe in these foolish old fairy stories."

"The *tomte* is not a foolish story," Erna insisted. "He is a friendly helper. He is—"

"Let me look at you. Just as I thought. Your ribs show. You should eat this porridge yourself."

Horrified, Erna shook her head. "I cannot eat what is for the *tomte*. He will box my ears."

Alfreda rolled her eyes. She had read books. She had read Swedish newspapers from America. Her sister, she decided, was as hopelessly ignorant as Olga and Helda and the other superstitious villagers. *What fools!* In America people behaved sensibly. They were educated and modern. They didn't spit on the floor to keep away evil spirits. They did not offer good food to an invisible man so that their cows would not go dry. "No one in America worries about having their ears boxed by imaginary creatures," Alfreda announced. "A *tomte* is nothing but ridiculous rot."

Erna clapped her hands over her ears. *I won't listen. I did not hear one word.*

"You'll be in big trouble if you hide out here all night. Grandfather wants you to come inside to say goodbye to our guests."

Erna took her hands from her ears. She wished her older sister would go away, back to the faraway place she'd come from.

Wind blew dust and chaff into the air and smarted Alfreda's eyes. "Better hurry, Erna."

Erna set her feet apart. She did not intend to leave until she had finished feeding the *tomte.*

She's a stubborn one. "Have you ever thought that your food offering might be for nothing?" Alfreda said, her eyes narrowing.

"What do you mean?"

"Perhaps your precious *tomte* isn't here anymore." Erna gulped.

"Perhaps he's deserted you."

Erna took a deep, trembling breath. "What are you saying?"

"If the *tomte* were here, wouldn't he have kept death away?" said Alfreda, unaware that she had just crushed inside her fist the sticky sweetmeats and the paper with the angels. She turned on her wooden heels. Without looking back to see if her sister was following her, she clattered *clunk-clunka-clunk* out the barn door.

Chapter 2

The next morning while Mama slept, Alfreda stacked the dirty dishes from the funeral guests. She made two trips carrying two buckets to their neighbor's pump for water. The water had to be heated in a kettle on the wood-burning stove. She poured the steaming water into a wooden tub to scrub the dishes. When she was finished, she used what was left of the soapy water to scrub the wooden floor in the *salong*, Grandmother's parlor that was ordinarily kept closed.

Against one wall in the small, dark room Alfreda found the cot that had been moved from the *skafferi* or kitchen pantry where Erna and Mama slept. It was Karl's cot, and it looked empty and forlorn. Someone had smoothed his favorite soft woolen blanket as if waiting for his return any moment.

He's gone. He's not coming back.

Alfreda bit her lip and wished she'd been kinder to Karl. She wished she had been able to spend more time with him. But how could she? She had been working so far away in Alna. Quickly she rubbed her eyes with her fists. She'd think of something else. Something pleasant.

On the bureau across the room were the America-pictures in bright frames decorated with little painted shells. None of these splendid people appeared sick or tired or overworked. They looked as satisfied and proud as rich Swedish gentry. These were the pictures of well-fed American aunts and uncles and cousins Alfreda had never met. They smiled confidently at her in their fancy clothing, big hats, and gleaming watch chains.

Alfreda picked up one of the pictures, careful not to leave a thumbprint on the polished glass. The photograph showed a man standing before impressive white-capped mountains. He wore suspenders and a broad-brimmed hat that cast a shadow over his forehead and eyebrows. It was impossible to tell if he was smiling, because his mustache was so thick and dark. Around his neck was a crisp white collar and an impressive tie. "California" was embossed in gold lettering in one corner.

Is this really Papa? Alfreda peered closer. But she could scarcely remember what her father looked like. She had certainly never seen Papa in such fine leather boots. The last time she laid eyes on him, he wore wooden shoes. He carried a bundle of clothing under an arm. When he leaned over and kissed her on the top of her head, he smelled spicy like tobacco and *brännvin*. She thought he was going north to the lumbering camps again. She never knew he was leaving for America. She never knew he was not coming back.

I wish I could go to America. Alfreda easily lifted the heavy bucket and placed it in the corner. Her arms were sinewy and tan from three years in hard service. She crouched on her hands and knees and began scrubbing. The scrub brush rasped and growled as she shoved it round and round, faster and faster. *In America I wouldn't have to slave for a lazy aunt. I could be free to do what I wanted. Just like Papa.*

She stood, hoisted the bucket, and tiptoed in her stocking feet out of the *salong,* closing the door behind her. Then she slipped her wooden clogs back on and walked outdoors to dump the dirty water under the gooseberry bush. *I can take care of myself. I'm strong enough.* For a moment she rested on the stone step. *In America I could be somebody. I could get a good education and become a teacher. No one would look down on me then.*

She listened to the hopeful song of an invisible lark singing high above the next field. In the distance a noisy flock of starlings landed in the budding birch trees. The demanding birds reminded her of her bossy aunt and all the work waiting for her. *Tomorrow.* Alfreda frowned. If only she had enough money to go to America. She'd never go back to Alna. Never.

Reluctantly she trudged inside the cottage and climbed up the ladder to the stuffy attic, where she'd slept the night before. Tacked to one sloping wall was a curling, yellowed poster that said: "The White Star Line. The Favorite Line of the Swedes! The World's Largest and Fastest Steamers!" She sat on the narrow bed and stared at the poster's enormous, proud steamship as it sliced through the waves. Modern, invincible. Bigger than anything else in the harbor. *To America. That's where it's going.*

Alfreda leaned forward, her elbows on her knees. She could imagine herself sailing away on that ship. She'd wear a glorious hat and carry a handbag of shiny oilcloth. Maybe she'd even have a muff for her hands and a fancy brooch pinned to her collar. She'd wear her hair differently, too. She'd buy some of those big wads of hair from the store. There was a special way to push these under her own hair so that her hair style stood up in the air. She'd look upper class and fine—just like the people in the America-pictures.

Suddenly she heard someone shouting in the kitchen below.

"Dagmar!" Grandfather called to Mama. "Wake up. There's a letter for you from America."

Alfreda scurried down the ladder in time to see Grandmother hobble in from the garden in her muddy apron. Erna leaned in the doorway and sucked a licorice stick, which could only have come from the store that very morning. She seemed more absorbed in her treat than the letter addressed to Mama. Alfreda found Erna's lack of interest irritating.

Mama rubbed her eyes, which were rimmed with dark circles. Her face was creased where it had lain against the fold of a blanket. She looked lost, bewildered as she opened the long white envelope.

"Who is it from?" demanded Grandfather, who could not read. "Is it Ivar?"

Mama nodded slowly.

Papa. Alfreda studied Mama's mouth carefully as she moved her lips, sounding out each word in silence.

Grandfather took a step closer. He licked his lips. "What's he say?"

Mama slowly lowered the letter into her lap. She burst into tears.

"Is he—is he sick?" Grandfather demanded. "Is he hurt?"

Mama let go of the letter. It floated to the floor. She buried her face in her hands.

Alfreda scrambled to pick up the letter. "I'll read it," she said and cleared her throat. She read aloud:

❧

"Dearest Wife and Family:

I must send some word so that you will know I am alive. Now I am in Chicago, where I have a job as a pipefitter. There is a good doctor here who says he knows where little Karl can get treatment for his lung ailment. I am sending you, dear wife, a ticket for yourself and our little son to come to America on the White Star Line and railroad tickets to Chicago. Later we will be able to send for the girls. How are they? I think of them often."

❧

Alfreda paused and bit her lip. Her voice trembled slightly as she continued:

❧

"America is a free land where there is no king and no meddlesome priests. I have worked at many different places. The most devilish job I have had was at a rolling mill in Pueblo, Colorado. I made good money— one hundred dollars a month. You must get ready and come this spring. My brother Fred will meet you in New York at a place called Ellis Island. Do not delay. This is all I have to say and I hope you understand me. I must end with many dear greetings to you. Greet my mother and father and all acquaintances. God bless you a safe voyage.

     Signed,
     Your loving husband and father,
     IVAR
     Chicago, U.S.A.

P.S. I advise you not to take a lot of linen cloth. Instead bring plenty of tinware. Pack down some food so that you have something to eat, in case you cannot stomach what they give you at sea. Hardtack is good; also some cheese and dried meat. Take along a food basket. When you arrive in America, there will be many who will approach you and offer you help. But you must watch your step. There are plenty of scoundrels ready to cheat the emigrant."

❧

"He doesn't know," Mama murmured.

No one spoke. It was so quiet in the kitchen, the only sound the bubbling of the coffeepot on the stove.

"Two tickets to America," Alfreda whispered. She shook from the envelope the two tickets printed with the words "White Star Line." She examined them closely, as if they might not be real. "We must go, Mama. You and I and the sewing machine."

Mama looked up at her and wiped her face with her sleeve. "What are you saying?"

"I can earn good money. So can you. One hundred dollars a month. Maybe more. We will send for Erna," Alfreda said, her voice filled with sudden hope. "She can stay here with Grandfather."

Erna crunched the last of her candy. She looked at Boppa. He stared at the floor as if deep in thought. Grandmother, who could not understand exactly what had happened, seemed to sense something tragic. She perched in her rocker and wept softly. "I will stay here," Erna said in a comforting voice as she patted Grandmother's shoulder. *I do not want to go to America.*

"Then it's settled," Alfreda said triumphantly. "Erna will wait behind. We'll make money and send for her. Then we can all be together."

Erna glanced curiously at her sister. Why did she want to go to America so badly? Nothing Erna knew about the faraway place appealed to her. *There are no* tomtar *in America. No little men. No magic forests. No cousins. No Boppa . . .*

Mama stood up slowly. For the first time she looked as if she were fully awake. "Alfreda, what about your employers—my sister and brother-in-law in Alna? We must write to them. We must tell them you will not be coming back."

Alfreda smiled. Great joy filled her heart. She could not think of anything to say. For the first time in three years she felt completely, utterly happy. *I am going to America.*

Erna turned and hurried out the door. She did not answer when Mama called, "Where do you think you're going?" She ran into the woods. Branches snapped in her face and tore at her clothing. She leaped over fallen trees and dodged past prickers. She did not know where she was running or why. She just had to get away from the cottage, from the choking, heavy air.

Don't they realize what they're doing? The idea of leaving was unbearable. *Yesterday. Has everyone already forgotten?* Little Karl all alone in a black box deep in the churchyard in the village. *If Mama goes to America, she will not be able to come to see him. Day and night he must lie there in the darkness. . . .*

Erna hurried into the little hut of branches and pieces of curled birch bark that she and her cousin Anna had built. She crawled inside and sat with her knees drawn up to her chest. She held her knees tightly against her chest and rocked back and forth, back and forth. Her heart galloped. *If they can leave poor little Karl so easily, what will they do when I die?*

"Hello, Erna?" a cheery voice called. It was her cousin. Anna's filthy upside-down face appeared in the opening of the little hut. Her red hair hung down in wild, thick tangles. "I see you. Do you think you're hiding?" She crawled inside and sat beside Erna. "What's the matter with your eyes? They're all red and watery," she asked and scratched her mosquito-bitten legs. "Are you sick?"

Erna did not answer.

"Is this the Silent Game?"

Erna shook her head. "My father sent America-tickets."

"Lucky!" Anna exclaimed. "For you?"

Erna shook her head again. "For my mother and Alfreda. I am to stay behind, and then they'll send for me when they make enough money."

Thoughtfully Anna scratched her legs some more. "You will make a long journey by yourself, do you know? When my uncle went, he had to take a wagon to Göteborg. Then he took the steamship across the North Sea to the English port of Hull. Then he had to travel on a railway train across England to some other place where he got on a steamship to New York. I know all this," she added wisely, "because I memorized his letter."

"Where is Chicago?" Erna demanded. "Is it far from New York?"

Anna shrugged. "Everything is far in America. America is very big. You must take plenty of food on your journey. My uncle said the ship's meat crawled with worms. Some passengers tried to steal his shoes. You must be tough and clever to travel to America."

Erna bit her lip. "I do not want to go."

"You mean, you don't want to go *alone?*"

"I don't want to go at all."

Anna looked at Erna in disbelief. "Everyone wants to go to America. That is where you go when you grow up."

Why couldn't her cousin understand? "Then I won't grow up," Erna announced. "I won't leave Boppa. I won't go to America."

Anna shook her head as if she thought Erna were very foolish. "Boppa is an old man. He will not live forever. What will become of you when he dies?"

Angry and shocked, Erna crawled out of the hut. She could not sit beside Anna another moment. She had to hurry back to the farm to make sure Boppa was all right.

"Where are you going?" Anna called to her.

Erna did not stop. She kept running. When she arrived back at the cottage, she could hear arguing voices, but she could not see her mother or her grandfather. On tiptoe she crept up to the open window and listened. Perhaps the grown-ups were changing their minds.

"The family must be together," Boppa said.

Good. We won't go.

"My son has not seen his children for seven years," Boppa continued. "This is a long, long time to be alone in a strange land."

"This money," Mama insisted, "is all you've saved for your own funeral."

Boppa is dying? Erna edged closer toward the open window. She peeked over the sill. Boppa looked the same as usual. His white hair stood up in tufts. His face was red as he waved his short arms in his usual, animated fashion.

"Pay the *kroner* back when you're able," Boppa told Mama. "There's just enough to buy one more ticket. Take Erna with you so that you can all be together again—"

Erna sank to her knees in Grandmother's bed of buttercups and bluebells. She could not believe her ears. *Take Erna with you.* What did he mean? How could he say such a horrible thing? *Doesn't he love me anymore?* Broken-hearted, she leaned against the cottage wall. How could Boppa be so cruel? How could he abandon her? Why was he sacrificing her for her father—someone she did not know or care about anymore? Slowly she sat on the ground, unaware of the flowers crushed beneath her. She buried her face in her hands and wept softly.

❧

March 19, 1912

Dearest Friend Maria Charlotta,

Forgive me for writing again so soon but I can never wait for a letter from you in America. I have some very important news. I am coming to Chicago, U.S.A. Today we received a letter from my father and he sends two tickets for the White Star Line! Can you find a job for me in a fine house? I must make as much money as I can so that I can go to school. I practice my English every day. I am so excited about the prospect of a new life in America, I will not be able to sleep tonight. It is my dream coming true at last. When I arrive in Chicago, will I recognize you? See how I can write some English words? I use the phrase book you gave me. **We had a parti last Sandi nait and de must fun we was nott mor and two girls but latse boys o wio just meck fam for erve day** How is that?

Your best new America-friend,
Alfreda

❧

Chapter

3

The matter was settled. Erna, Alfreda, and Mama would leave the next day on a wagon for the port city of Göteborg. No one asked Erna if she wanted to go to America. Her opinion wasn't important. There were preparations and packing to be done, so no one noticed when Erna pouted. No one cared when she purposefully kicked over a bucket of fresh drinking water. Everyone was too busy to scold her.

"Alfreda, bring that chest down carefully," Mama commanded. "The one for the linens. And don't forget—" She stood in the middle of the kitchen, her finger to her cheek. What was she trying to remember? Her hair had come undone

29

and flew about in white-yellow strands around her face. She seemed almost like a giddy young girl. "It's a good thing Ivar sold the farm when he did," she said gaily. "We can be on our way without waiting to find someone to buy the place."

Alfreda watched her mother curiously. *Strange.* Mama made it sound as if the sale of the place were the smartest thing Papa ever did. *Doesn't she remember?* The day Papa sold their small farm to Olaf Jans, Mama cried as if her heart would break. And now cattle grazed on their three miserable acres and the empty house had collapsed in on itself like a rotten pumpkin.

Mama folded linen and stacked each piece carefully on the table. As she worked, she softly sang a song. A silly song about a boy taking his girlfriend for a ride on his new bicycle. Alfreda had never heard Mama sing that song before. She helped Mama scour the old oak clothes chest from the attic.

"There!" Mama said, wiping her forehead. She examined the enormous chest that was nearly five feet long and three feet wide. It had belonged to Papa's family for so many years, no one knew exactly how old it was. At each end were iron handles. In the front was a big iron clasp that closed the chest and locked it tight. "That's better. Clean as new."

The America-chest reminded Erna of a coffin. *It's big enough for me to fit inside with room to spare.*

"What should we take? What should we leave behind?" Mama asked. Her voice was half-question, half-answer. She carefully lowered her precious sewing machine into the America-chest.

"It is cold in America. As cold as Sweden," Grandfather said.

Mama cradled the sewing machine with plenty of woolen clothing. She packed her knitting needles, woolen and linen yarns, needles, and thread of all kinds. Alfreda tucked camphor and sweet lavender around bedclothes, sheets, and blankets so that they would not smell mildewed on the long trip.

In a roomy willow basket—the same kind Papa suggested in his letter—Grandmother generously emptied her larder. She wrapped and packed eight loaves of rye bread, a wooden tub of strongly salted butter, a whole cheese, half a dozen smoked sausages, a piece of salt pork, a dozen salted herrings. She also tucked away a pound of coffee, a pound of sugar, a bag of dried apples, and small cloth bags containing salt and pepper.

"This is too much food," Mama protested when she saw all the delicacies that Grandmother had given them.

Grandmother waved her hand as if to motion her to be quiet.

Mama gathered together medicines for the trip: Hoffman's Heart-Aiding Drops, the Prince's Drops, and a gallon of wormwood-seed *brännvin* guaranteed to cure seasickness. She handed Erna and Alfreda each a small bag with a long, looped string attached. Erna sniffed the bag, which smelled strongly of camphor. "What's this for?"

"To prevent seasickness," Mama replied. "Wear it around your neck."

Grandmother gave Alfreda a pot of soft soap so that they could keep clean on the journey, some phosphor salve, and a fine-tooth steel comb. "And this?" Alfreda asked, holding up the comb.

"Lice," Mama replied.

"There are lice in America?" Alfreda said. She could not imagine anything so nasty existing in such a perfect place.

"On the ship," Mama replied, "there will be many people from other countries."

"Oh," Alfreda said as if Mama's explanation made perfect sense. *Other people from other countries have lice. Not Americans.*

"But what should we do about the scoundrels that Papa mentioned?" Alfreda asked. "They sounded dangerous."

Grandfather showed Alfreda the other special sheepskin bag that he had made for Mama to hide their money, identification papers, White Star Line steamship tickets, and railway tickets. "Dagmar, wear this next to your body so that no one will steal from you," he told Mama.

"It itches," Mama protested. She scratched her neck. Already there were red blisters on her skin. Whenever she was nervous, these skin irritations appeared.

"Wear the bag anyway," Grandfather insisted.

Alfreda packed her own private bundle of clothing that she would carry herself. Another dress, a change of underwear, some stockings. There wasn't much. Her most important belonging was a book of English and Swedish phrases her best friend Maria Charlotta had given her before she left for America. The book was called *Utvandrarens Tolk* or *The Emigrant's Interpreter*. It was filled with all kinds of good advice she'd need for their long voyage.

Erna watched all this frantic activity with distaste and sadness. Mama and Alfreda thought they were packing everything that was essential.

But what about the really important things they were leaving behind—things they couldn't fit into the America-chest? What about the wild raspberry bush behind the barn where she and Karl used to pick sweet fruit? What about the mud daubers who sang under the eaves? What about the salmon-colored clouds that appeared in the pale blue dawn sky? None of these most important things would fit in the America-chest.

Erna slipped out the door into the fresh air. No one would notice if she left. *No one cares about me.* She roamed through the woods, waving a branch of pussy willow over each favorite secret spot. The rock shaped like a sleeping giant. The tree with the secret hollow place for special rocks and messages.

Everyone had been so busy getting ready, Boppa had not spoken to her all day. Sadly she returned to the farm and shuffled inside the barn. She sat on the worn floor in a pool of sunshine. She took a deep breath and tried to memorize the warm, safe aroma. She tried to memorize the way the delicious light bathed her arms and face. No barn would feel so familiar. *Tomte, where are you?* She sat quietly, hoping that the farm's little guardian would come out and reveal himself to her. Perhaps he would say goodbye.

She waited and waited. The cow lowed. The horse made dull, hollow thuds with his hooves. But the *tomte* never came out of hiding.

Discouraged, Erna stood up. She looked up in the loft where she and Karl had tied a swing. She hungrily tried to recall the day that she and her brother found the mouse family in the hay. How happy Karl had been! And then there was the evening Crazy Ole tramped past while they were hiding in the barn and nearly scared them to death with his strange howling.

"What are you doing here, dear child?" Boppa called.

His bright voice made her jump.

"Nothing," she said and quickly knuckled under each eye so he wouldn't see her tears.

He cleared his throat the way he always did when he was going to say something important. Something she must remember. "You understand, do you, why I gave your mother the *kroner* for your steamship ticket?"

Miserably Erna shook her head. She could not look at him. She knew she would start crying again.

"A sacrifice—a real sacrifice—is giving up something cherished and precious that one loves more than anything in the world," he said softly. "Do you know what I mean?"

Erna nodded, but she did not really understand. "Boppa, don't send me to America," she pleaded. "I want to stay here with you."

Grandfather took a deep breath. "You must understand that I make this sacrifice for my son, your father. He loves you, too."

Erna bit her lip. She did not care about Papa's feelings. She did not even remember him.

"Someday you'll understand," Grandfather continued. "Maybe not now. Maybe in many years."

Erna refused to reply. Somehow she could sense that this conversation hurt Boppa deeply. *Can he feel as miserable as I do?* She couldn't help herself, but she felt strangely powerful.

"I have something for you," Grandfather said slowly. He handed her a small object wrapped in a piece of wrinkled brown paper and tied with a string. "Do not unwrap it until you are on your way. Until you can no longer see the farm anymore."

Erna turned the little gift over and over in her hands. "Thank you, Boppa," she mumbled. When she looked up at him, he had already turned and was limping slowly toward the house. At that moment she knew. *I'll never see him again.*

*　　*　　*

The next day Mama hired a driver with a cart to take them to Göteborg. Early in the morning they loaded their belongings and the America-chest on the cart. Old Klinta-Kitta, Olga, Helda, Olaf, and all the other villagers and cousins came with garlands of flowers for Alfreda, Erna, and their mother.

"You are so lucky! Will you write to me?" Anna demanded.

Erna nodded. She did not want to cry in front of her cousin. *I wish it was you that was going. Not me.* As bravely as she could, she smiled at Anna and hugged her. Uncomfortably Erna adjusted the overpoweringly sweet garlands of lilac and lily of the valley. *These flowers are funeral flowers.*

"Farewell!" shouted Alfreda. Triumphantly she climbed into the wagon. *I am leaving forever!*

Mama, who had worried all morning about the sewing machine, climbed into the wagon after checking the America-chest one last time. The red rash had begun to spread up her neck and down her arms. All the same, she waved cheerfully to the neighbors.

Erna felt very alone, very tragic after she kissed Boppa and climbed into the wagon, too. Grandmother dabbed her eyes with the corner of her apron. Boppa had his arm around Grandmother, who was sobbing louder now. Their faces seemed to say, "This place belongs to us. We belong to this place." They would never leave Sweden.

The driver shouted to the horse, and the wagon rolled forward. Anna and the villagers cheered and waved. At that moment Erna could hardly resist the impulse to run into the woods one last time. What did she care if she made her sister and mother miss the steamship? *It would serve them right.* In the distance church bells tolled. Erna whispered a little prayer for her brother, knowing she would never visit his grave again. Sadly she watched her grandparents become smaller and smaller until they finally seemed to disappear.

When she could no longer see the farm, she took Boppa's gift from her pocket.

"What's that?" Alfreda demanded.

"A little keepsake Anna gave me," Erna lied. She didn't want to make her sister more irritable and jealous if she found out Boppa had given her something special.

Alfreda looked critically at the crumpled paper in Erna's hands. "Well, don't lose it," she warned. "We won't have time to look for misplaced souvenirs."

Erna frowned. *What she's really saying is that if I*

get lost, she won't bother to find me, either. As soon
as her sister looked away, Erna unwrapped the
package. A small pine wood carving of a man
with a wise, mysterious smile and a big nose. He
wore a pointed hat. Boppa had made the *tomte*,
she could tell. She squeezed the wooden figure,
hoping that her sister would never find it and
make fun of her. She smiled and tucked the carving inside her pocket. *Alfreda's wrong. Soon there
will be* tomte *in America.*

After a long, uncomfortable ride, they finally
arrived in the port city of Göteborg. A large,
rusty ship called the *Tasso* sat in the harbor.
"That's it," the wagon driver said. "Your ship."

Worry clouded Mama's face. "Will such a
rattletrap ship float all the way across the North
Sea to England?"

"That is not my problem," replied the driver.
He dragged the America-chest from the back of
the wagon and dumped it unceremoniously onto
the ground.

For the first time Mama looked as if she might
cry. "Could you not treat our possessions more
gently?"

The driver seemed eager to leave them. Alfreda
made sure they had all their belongings. Then she
counted their money twice before she paid the

driver his fare. She read a sign on the dock. "We will board the ship later today," she said with authority.

Mama did not contradict her. Slowly she sat down on the America-chest and scratched her arms absentmindedly. "We cannot carry all our belongings through town," she said. "We cannot leave anything here. Someone might steal my sewing machine."

"Are you all right, Mama?" Erna asked.

"I am fine," Mama replied in a dull voice.

"Erna and I will see about the ship at the ticket office," Alfreda suggested. "Mama, you wait here."

Mama barely nodded. For the second time she was allowing Alfreda to make the decisions. This seemed strange to Erna, who was accustomed to Mama behaving in a much more forceful manner. Reluctantly Erna followed her sister.

Alfreda felt secretly exhilarated by the prospect of their voyage—even though the *Tasso* looked like a leaky tub. "Come along!" she said to her poky sister. *Must Erna dawdle so? How I wish I were traveling alone!*

Erna was unaccustomed to walking on cobblestones. In their little village the roads were made of dirt. The Göteborg cobblestones seemed to grab the heels of Erna's wooden shoes and made her stumble. But Alfreda would not wait. She hurried along, her shoes called *knock knocka knock* against the street as if she'd hurried along this way hundreds of times. Wagons careened past. Peddlers called to them, but Alfreda never stopped, never paused.

After waiting in line an interminable amount of time at the Wilson Line office, Alfreda secured the information they needed from the Wilson Line agent. The *Tasso* would leave early that evening. They had not arrived a moment too soon. "Come along, slowpoke!" she said to Erna and hurried back to Mama the way they'd come.

Erna was tired. Her feet hurt. She was hungry and thirsty. And she needed to find a privy. But her sister would not slow down long enough for her to find a place to go to the bathroom. Alfreda did not seem to care that Erna was lagging farther and farther behind. "Can we stop? Please?" Erna pleaded. Irritated, Alfreda agreed to allow Erna to lean against a hitching post on the street to catch her breath. The smell of rotting garbage that washed down the gutter was so terrible, she did not dare breathe. "Let's go," Erna said finally.

When the time came to board the *Tasso*, Mama

spent a long time arguing with the crew about the fate of the America-chest. She wanted to make sure it would be safe, that no one would drop it. "If we had a man along, we would not be treated so badly," Mama said under her breath as they began to walk up the treacherous, bouncing gangplank.

"You have been without a man for seven years and done very well for yourself," Alfreda replied in a matter-of-fact voice. She hoisted the wicker basket in her arms and marched inside the ship.

Mama shot a glance at her bold daughter but said nothing. Back home, Erna knew, Alfreda would have been punished for such impertinence. But not here. Not on their way to America when so much depended on Alfreda's energy and resourcefulness. Her boundless determination frightened Erna a little. *I could never be like her.* Nervously she adjusted the bag of clothing she had flung over her shoulder and made sure the little *tomte* was safe inside her pocket.

Chapter 4

The third-class accommodations deep inside the *Tasso* were simply two large rooms. One was for women, the other for men. Against the walls were groupings of four bunks partitioned from the main area by a mildewed piece of canvas.

"What is this doing here?" Erna asked. Around her feet was a thick layer of wood shavings and sawdust. The familiar, piney smell reminded her of Boppa's workshop.

"Perhaps some construction under way," Alfreda announced. She pulled back a smaller piece of canvas curtain. "Here are our beds."

"But there are four beds and only three of us," Erna said nervously. "That means we shall have to share with a stranger. I don't want to sleep with a stranger."

"Can't be helped," Alfreda said. *Spoiled brat. What did she expect, some luxury ship?*

"I think I'll just lie down for a while," Mama said wearily. She began to fuss with the bed. "Where is the mattress?"

All that could be seen on the bunk's hard slatted wooden surface were several folded gray wool blankets. There were no sheets.

"Can't be any worse than the hard cot I slept on in Aunty's cold, drafty kitchen," Alfreda said.

Mama began to whimper all the same.

"Now what's wrong?" Alfreda demanded.

Mama unfolded the blankets and showed Alfreda. Dried, squashed bodies of vermin lodged between the folds.

"Well," Alfreda said cheerfully, "at least they're dead."

Mama moaned and sat on the edge of the bed, her head in her hands. She scratched her neck and her cheeks and said nothing.

"Here are your metal plates, your spoons, your forks, your cups," said a man who briskly shoved a pile of eating utensils through the canvas flap. "This woman will sleep in the extra bunk."

An old woman, bent and dirty, pushed her way

through the canvas flap clutching a battered bundle. With blue, weepy eyes the old woman gazed suspiciously at Alfreda, Mama, and Erna. She did not say one word as she crawled determinedly into the lowest bunk—as if she intended to stay there the entire voyage. The smell of urine rising from the old woman was so strong, Erna gagged. Mama's hand went to her face.

"Let's go above deck," Alfreda suggested. Before Mama could protest that they should be wary of leaving any of their belongings, the two girls hurried up the steep stairwell to fresh air on the deck above. Mama followed them as they crept to the rail and stared out at the port of Göteborg.

"Does the ship always move so much when it is supposed to be still?" Erna demanded.

Alfreda nodded wisely. "You see those waves? They cause the ship to rock the way it does. There is nothing dangerous in that."

Erna looked down at the gray-green water that splashed against the metal ship's hull. *I wish I could swim.* She did not want to mention her fears to Alfreda, who seemed so brave and fearless. Suddenly the crew began shouting to one another. Men scrambled along the deck and untied thick ropes. A great rush of steam went up from the enormous smokestack on the *Tasso*.

"What are they saying?" Mama demanded. "I can't understand a word!" She held her hands to her ears with the next piercing blast of steam and the shriek of a whistle.

"They are speaking English!" Alfreda shouted back.

Erna listened to the sailors. She had never heard so much English before. Their tinny chatter reminded her of the sounds angry squirrels made in the woods back home. *I'll never master such a foreign tongue.*

The ship began to move slowly away from shore. The acrid smell of smoke from the belching smokestack filled Erna's nose and made her sneeze. Mama held a handkerchief to her face. But none of them wanted to go back down into the hold, where the air was even worse. They stayed on the deck as the Swedish coastline slowly began to waver and vanish.

A bell gonged. "Dinner time!" a sailor shouted in Swedish.

"Now we can eat," Alfreda said. In the west she watched the sun setting and the small bright points of light that were the first stars appearing. The wind had picked up and was cold and biting.

When Alfreda tried to take a few steps, she stumbled but quickly righted herself. *I'll need some practice to learn to walk properly on a ship.*

Mama clutched the railing as if she might fly overboard at any moment. She moved carefully, placing one foot in front of the other. Her face was greenish and her lips had disappeared, sucked inside her mouth as if by doing so she might increase her concentration.

Erna followed her mother and sister down the steep steps into the eating area, which was hot and steamy with the smell of unwashed bodies and mysterious gray boiled meat. Alfreda read the crude menu someone had written in Swedish on the wall:

"Sunday: half pound beef, porridge or
pudding, dried fruit
Monday: pork, pea soup or boiled cabbage
Tuesday: beef, gruel or peas
Wednesday: beef, rice and molasses
Thursday: beef, porridge or pudding,
dried fruit
Friday: beef, pork, pea soup or dried fruit
Saturday: herring or fish, peas or
brown beans."

"Don't believe that sign," a woman said, elbowing Alfreda to hurry along in line. "They give us what they wish. Stale white rusk biscuits, rancid butter. And don't forget coffee in the morning and tea in the evening."

"Slops in the morning and evening you mean," another Swedish woman said and snorted. "The English can't make decent coffee, and their tea tastes like mop water."

Alfreda retreated out of earshot of the grumbling women. She handed a plate to her sister and mother and listened to the other passengers around her who babbled in a confusion of Norwegian and Swedish and Danish and English. The steerage passengers crowded around the hot stove where the food was ladled onto their plates and then shuffled back though the sawdust to a long table where they ate quickly before their meals slid down the table with the next lurch of a wave. Some of the men stood up on wobbly legs and made toasts. Others clinked their cups and drank heartily. Shoulder to shoulder they sat and ate their food and drank and shouted *"Skaal"* so often that Alfreda's ears hurt.

Mama did not eat her pale, boiled dinner or her chunk of stale, black bread. At the last moment she stood up and hurried away, back in the direction of the slop buckets the women used as a makeshift privy behind a canvas curtain.

"What's wrong with Mama?" Erna asked.

"She's seasick. Nothing serious," replied Alfreda, who ate with gusto. "She'll be fine in no time."

Mama was not fine, though. For the next thirty-six hours, the *Tasso* bucked and plunged across the North Sea straight into westerly winds and enormous, rolling waves. Tossed like grain during threshing, everyone in steerage soon became ill. There were no more shouts of *"Skaal!"* No more boastings of gold mines in America and sausage shops owned by uncles so wealthy that their teeth were capped with silver. No. Now Erna and Alfreda learned the real reason for the sawdust on the ship's floor. It was to collect the growing puddles of vomit from the passengers. Every morning, the old sawdust was shoveled away and fresh was sprinkled in its place.

All night Erna lay in the bunk and clutched the little bag of camphor around her neck. *Will the ocean never stop pitching and crashing?* She felt so sick, she thought she might die. Her stomach never stopped heaving, even when there was nothing left inside. Her only comfort was the little *tomte*, who kept smiling no matter what happened.

In the bunk below her she could hear the old woman groaning and becoming sicker by the moment. Her smell was so awful that Erna became even more ill. In her delirium she thought angrily of Boppa. *This is all his fault. How could he make me suffer so?*

Even Mama, who had once seemed so light-hearted when news of their trip began, now could not speak or crawl. She lay in the foul-smelling darkness and wept and groaned, unable even to swallow a tiny sip of wormwood-seed *brännvin*.

Only Alfreda was able to stumble from the bunk, dodging damp, foul piles of sawdust. She clambered up the steps into the windy night. The fresh air filled her nose, and for once she felt as if she could really breathe. She looked in all directions and could see no light that indicated the horizon. After a long search around the deck, she found a corner out of the wind and wrapped herself in a mildewed tarp and fell asleep.

At first light there was a shout. Alfreda's eyes flew open. Someone stood over her. He chuckled to his friend and said something in English. Angrily Alfreda struggled to her feet. She could not understand the two unshaven sailors, but she could tell by their expressions that they were making fun of her. One of them reached out as if to grab her. She gave his wrist a quick twist and, to his amazement, sent him hurling off balance.

"Get away from me, you swine!" she hissed. Then, using the first English phrase she could think of, she screamed, *"This miht is badd, vi cannat iht itt."*

The fallen man and his companion burst into laughter.

Alfreda blushed, pulled herself to her feet, and hurried away. She was determined to practice diligently from *The Emigrant's Interpreter* so that she would never be humiliated in this way again. Before she could escape back into the hold, a mob of weary steerage passengers blocked the stairway. One of them emerged and pointed to a low, dark smudge on the western horizon. "England!"

Alfreda stood at the railing and peered in the distance. Other passengers joined her.

"No mountains!" a Swede said, definitely unimpressed.

"No fjords. No trees," another agreed. "What kind of flat, featureless place is this?"

"Didn't our forefathers, the Vikings, conquer this place?" the Swede boasted. "England can hold nothing to the beauty of our homeland."

Soon the bragging began in earnest. The sickness of the night before seemed forgotten. Small flasks appeared and the men on deck began toasting each other *"Skaal"* and shouting jokes and stories.

Alfreda turned and saw her little sister weakly pulling herself up on deck. Erna looked so small, thin, and pale. She blinked in the bright sunlight as she stumbled to Alfreda. "Where is Mama?" Alfreda demanded.

"Below," Erna replied.

"Your face is dirty," Alfreda said, handing her a handkerchief dampened with spit.

"Can't help it. I've been sick all night." Erna wiped her cheeks. She peered in the distance. She could see the growing mass of land, but she did not feel any excitement. She felt only weariness. "How far to America?"

"The trip from England to America across the Atlantic is still hundreds and hundreds of miles. Many times farther and rougher than the trip across the North Sea. The trip we just made was nothing in comparison."

"Nothing?" Erna replied in disbelief. *How will I survive?*

Alfreda, her sister, and Mama anxiously waited to reach shore. When the *Tasso* finally anchored

in the harbor, they could see and smell the smoky
city of Hull. Customs officials came out to the
steamship on a smaller boat and climbed aboard
to check the passenger list. Customs inspection
was merely a formality, Alfreda could see that as
well as anyone. The Swedes, Danes, and Norwe-
gians were herded from the docks and then
driven up into huge horse-drawn vans to haul
them to the railroad station with all their
worldly belongings.

Mama fretted endlessly about their America-
chest. Was it all right? Had anything happened
to the sewing machine? What if it were broken?
How would they ever make the money they
needed to live? She asked these questions over
and over until Alfreda thought she might go mad.

"Be quiet, Mama," Alfreda scolded. "The
America-chest has been loaded in the back of the
wagon. I saw it."

Erna looked at her sister with surprise. Even
more amazing was the fact that Mama ignored
Alfreda's comment. She was too busy observing
a group of English men and women. "See how
they look at us!" Mama whispered.

The men carried sticks and umbrellas under
their arms and the women had enormous hats
with dead birds perched on their brims. The En-

glish folk wore gloves even though it was not winter. They laughed and pointed at Erna and her sister and mother in the van as if they looked as incredible as the two-headed goat Erna had seen once when a circus came through the village.

"English swine!" Alfreda hissed in Swedish.

"Alfreda!" Mama said in horror. "What if the gentry hears such disrespect? What if the English sheriff drags us away to jail?"

"Those rich folk can't understand what I just said," Alfreda said contemptuously. "They can't speak Swedish any better than I can speak English. But I don't plan on remaining stupid for long."

Erna shot her sister a sideways glance.

"I am going to spend all my time on our voyage learning to speak English," Alfreda continued. "Then I will teach you, too."

"I prefer Swedish," Mama said proudly.

"I don't really want to learn English, either," Erna said in a small voice. "It sounds like animal talk to me."

Alfreda laughed harshly. "If you wish not to be treated like a beast, you must learn what the Americans are saying."

Erna sank lower into the seat. *She wants us to*

forget everything Swedish. The wooden wagon seat was hard and uncomfortable, and it jolted and bumped over the English road. When the wagon finally stopped, she stepped on the ground and felt immediately some kind of strangeness overtake her. The English houses were tall and made of brick. At home the houses were made of wood with thatched roofs. She saw a small, scraggly tree and a patch of flowers caged inside a cold, metal fence. The tree and grass looked familiar. But everything else seemed dreamlike and odd — from the English street signs she couldn't read to the drivers' shouts she couldn't understand.

"Isn't this wonderful?" Alfreda exclaimed, surveying all the crowds and confusion of the railway station. "Our first railroad trip."

Erna shook her head doubtfully. Mama scratched her arms and neck. The rash had spread across her face. She tried to hide it with a kerchief, which she wore so that her cheeks were covered. "Do you think the train is safe?" Mama demanded.

Alfreda coughed from the coal dust that seemed to float everywhere in the noisy station. She took her mother by the elbow and her sister by the hand and helped them up the enormous step that led inside the belching, enormous train. In the pit of her stomach Alfreda was scared, too. But she did not wish anyone to know it. Skillfully she guided Mama and Erna to the third-class train car where they had been directed.

Inside the emigrant railway car were seats in a row. Alfreda ran her hand over the soft upholstery on one of the seats that lined the walls of the long, narrow railway car—nothing like the dark, crowded hold of the *Tasso*. The comfortable-looking seats seemed too fine, too fancy for third class. Windows on either side of the narrow room gave a view of the outside. All this glass must have cost much money, Alfreda decided. *Maybe we're in the wrong railway car.*

Other noisy emigrants scrambled aboard with bundles and baskets and squalling babies. They pushed and shoved and took their places on the seats. Alfreda decided that she and her sister and mother should do the same before there was nowhere left for them. "Sit here," she told Erna and Mama.

Mama seemed too terrified to sit by the window. "I don't want to see where we're going," she said. "I don't want anyone to notice me through the window and make fun of me." Shyly she pulled her kerchief around her face as best she could. She gripped her hands in her lap over her bundle so tightly that her knuckles turned white.

Erna sat beside her, wide-eyed with wonder and terror. *What will happen next?* It seemed impossible that anything could be strong enough to pull this enormously heavy steel train—bigger than any wagon she'd ever seen before. Evil clouds of steam floated past. The train hissed. Erna felt as if she might be sick any moment. She held the *tomte* tight and prayed she would not vomit on her sister and cause her to become enraged.

Suddenly a whistle pierced the air with an awful sound—worse than the howl of a troll or the dying shriek of a giant in the mountains. Erna covered her ears with her hands. *I must get off this dangerous machine.* When she stood up, Alfreda grabbed her and pulled her back into the seat. "Sit down," Alfreda commanded.

Chapter

5

Before Erna could escape, the station began to move. She watched in amazement as the people and the steel poles and the luggage wagons slipped backward as if in slow motion. "The train station's floating away!" she whispered to her sister.

"No, it's not!" Alfreda insisted. *"We're* moving. The train is leaving the station."

Mama kept her eyes closed tightly as if she were praying.

The train rocked and rumbled and purred and soon the station disappeared. The windows filled with a kind of gray-white overcast light. The train moved faster and faster, and the fences and dirty buildings flew past at such a dizzying speed that Alfreda was certain at any moment they'd go hurling into a hard, brick wall and be smashed to pieces.

"Look at that!" Alfreda said. She pointed. The pall of smoke belching from chimneys and factory was thick and choking. "How do these English people breathe?"

Erna settled back in her seat and tried to force herself to relax. She was exhausted. The rhythmic, rolling movement of the train was preferable to the unpredictable lurching of the *Tasso*. She'd like to forget that horrible feeling of her stomach heaving and her ears pounding. She closed her eyes and listened to the *clickety-clack clickety-clack*.

Alfreda glanced over at her sister, whose head bobbed to one side. *Good. She's going to sleep. She needs some rest.* Alfreda could not sleep. Everything she saw out the window was too wonderful and new. The view had turned bright green now, and the English countryside was lit with a few rays of sunshine that had managed to escape through the gray clouds overhead, dramatically illuminating the distant fields.

Green walls edged the English fields. Alfreda had never seen anything like them. At first she thought the walls were made of rocks covered by moss. But, no. How could that be? Each side appeared to be uniformly covered. *Whoosh!* A wall flew past the window and she looked at it carefully in the split second that it passed. It was a bush. Some kind of English bush. What a strange idea! These English planted the edge of each field with shrubs. At home men built fences from piles of rocks hauled laboriously from the fields. *Some poor English serving girl probably tends these bushes.* She watched the patterns of English hedges fly past until her eyelids grew heavy. Soon she had nodded off, too.

The train rumbled through the countryside, stopping every so often at several junctions that required Mama, Alfreda, and Erna and the other passengers bound for Southampton to change trains.

Finally, late in the afternoon, the emigrant train rolled into the station at Southampton. This station was even bigger and more crowded than the one at Hull.

"This way! This way!" Alfreda called impatiently to Mama and Erna, who teetered under the burden of their belongings.

Erna's legs felt wobbly as she tried to regain her balance on solid ground again. Somehow she could not rid the sound and hum of the train from her ears.

Wandering up and down between the tracks were men wearing caps with the insignias of various transatlantic lines. They smiled in a pleasant way that somehow made Alfreda feel reassured. She waved to one with a white star on his cap.

"*Star White?*" she said to him.

He nodded and made a little amused bow. Then he pointed with one finger as if to say, "This way."

Mama pulled frantically on Alfreda's sleeve. "What about our America-chest? What if it is lost?"

Alfreda stopped and pulled her America-phrase book from her pocket and scanned it desperately. All she could find in the section called "At the Railroad" were:

May I offer you a cigar?

Shall we not open the vindow?

None of these seemed correct. Desperately she used sign language. She pointed to another person lugging a heavy trunk. Then she pointed to herself and her mother.

The man with the White Star cap nodded reassuringly. He said something to Alfreda that she could not understand. He kept walking.

"Where is he going? What will happen to my sewing machine?" Mama sobbed hysterically. She looked as if she might crumple up right there on the train platform like the newspaper scraps that blew past their feet and lodged on the tracks.

Erna shot a nasty glance at Alfreda. Her sister did not notice. Alfreda called to the man with the White Star cap, desperate that he would abandon them. *Then we'll be lost here for hours. Perhaps we'll even miss the steamship.*

The White Star cap seemed to be deep in conversation with another White Star cap. They pointed at Alfreda, Erna, and Mama. The second White Star cap approached them. Alfreda was relieved to hear that the second fellow could speak English *and* Swedish. He told them he could translate for them. Politely he showed them the building where they would find the White Star Line office and infirmary.

"Infirmary?" Alfreda asked, not liking the ominous sound of the word. "What is that?"

"The place where the doctor takes a look at you before you board. He makes sure you are well," the Swedish White Star cap said.

"We are all well," Alfreda said stubbornly. "Nothing is wrong with any of us."

"It is only a precaution," he said. "If you get

all the way to America, they will do the same. And if you are not well, they will keep you at Ellis Island for months and not let you leave. Worse yet, they'll send you home. It's better to make sure here in Southampton that you do not have a heart tremor or an eye problem."

Alfreda looked at the man suspiciously. How could she be sure he was telling her the truth?

"Is he talking about Mama?" Erna whispered to her sister.

Alfreda glanced at Mama out of the corner of her eye. Mama scratched her arms. Suddenly Alfreda felt worried. Would the White Star doctor find something serious in Mama's rash? She followed him to the office and stood in line at the counter with Grandfather's money tied inside a handkerchief.

"I have two tickets on the White Star line," Alfreda said with translation help from the Swedish White Star cap. "I need one more."

"Sorry, no ships are leaving. There's a coal strike in Southampton," the oily clerk said.

Alfreda stared at the man in disbelief. "You must be mistaken. We have come a very, very long way. Our father bought two tickets on the White Star Line. The ship is to leave tomorrow.

Do you see?" Her hand trembled as she pushed the tickets through the window.

The clerk inspected the tickets.

"What is wrong?" Mama whined. "Is something wrong?"

"Shhhhh!" Alfreda hissed at her mother. She stood on tiptoe and spoke in a clear, firm voice so that the Swedish White Star cap would translate each word. "I will not be turned away."

"There is no ship. Sorry," the clerk said and winked at her.

In exasperation she took a deep breath. "Look harder."

The other White Star cap gave Alfreda an admiring glance, then whispered something to the clerk. "There is one other ship," the translator explained. "A few berths are left in steerage."

"Three berths?"

"Yes. It's the *Titanic*," the clerk said. "A brand-new ship. It leaves at noon tomorrow on its first voyage. The newspapers have all been talking about it. They call it the unsinkable ship."

Mama crept closer. She yanked on Alfreda's sleeve as insistent as a young child. "I don't like the idea of a first voyage," she whispered. "What if something goes wrong?"

"Nothing will go wrong," Alfreda hissed.

Mama narrowed her eyes. "Calling a ship un-sinkable flies in the face of God. Isn't there an-other ship? Something else?"

A fat man standing behind Alfreda, her sister, and mother began pushing and speaking in a complaining voice. Alfreda refused to be hurried. She asked the clerk again if there was another ship.

He shook his head. "Take this or nothing, miss. The *Titanic* is the only ship leaving the harbor. It's on a tight schedule and is using the coal that would ordinarily have gone for the other steam-ships."

The fat man tapped his foot.

"We'll take it," Alfreda said. She pushed the precious money under the window grating.

The clerk made a loud noise stamping more pieces of paper. "Take these to the infirmary. A doctor will make sure you can sail. Don't be late. The *Titanic* will leave promptly."

Eagerly Alfreda gathered up the necessary pa-pers. She thanked the Swedish White Star cap. Mama and Erna followed on Alfreda's heels as she escaped the growing crowd around the ticket counter.

"Where do we go now? What happens next?" Mama demanded.

"The doctor," Alfreda said.

Mama looked worried. But she followed her older daughter into the building, where they were inspected by two haughty women in white uniforms. Their clothes were inspected for lice. Their heads were checked for nits. One woman who came out of the building was not so lucky. She ducked in embarrassment and adjusted her kerchief to hide her shaven head. "I hope that doesn't happen to me," Erna said softly.

The doctor peered into Erna's and Alfreda's eyes. He listened to their hearts with a strange long black snakelike object. Alfreda and Erna passed the examination without any problems. But when it was Mama's turn to be examined, she became hysterical. Back home, going to the doctor meant certain death was imminent. It took much convincing by Alfreda to get Mama to walk into the doctor's office. The nurse had to practically drag her the last few feet. The door slammed shut.

A few minutes later, when she emerged again, she was sobbing.

"What's wrong?" Alfreda demanded in an anxious voice.

"My skin!" Mama said, gulping for air. "He

said I cannot go to America on the ship until my rash goes away."

Alfreda leaned against the wall, stunned. *Now what?* "How much money do we have?"

Mama sniffed. "Not enough for all three of us to find food and lodging for long enough for my skin to clear. Not enough to get home, either. The doctor said I can stay at the Swedish Travelers' Aid Society until I am better. Or we can go back to Sweden."

Alfreda scowled. More than ever she wished she were traveling alone. She wouldn't have to worry about anyone except herself. She took a deep breath. They had come so far. She couldn't bear the idea of going home. *A failure.* She'd never get a second chance to escape. She was so close. She could not give up now. "I'm going to America," she announced. "I will take Erna with me. Mama, you can stay here, get well, and come over on the next ship. You can exchange this ticket for another one sailing later."

Slowly Mama nodded her head. "We have no other choice," she said sadly.

Erna curled her fists. She wanted to punch her bossy sister. Why did she have to make all the decisions? It wasn't fair. No one asked Erna what she wanted to do. She didn't want to go with

Alfreda because she didn't trust her. She didn't want to stay with Mama, either. She did not like this place. She did not like these unfriendly, jabbering English people. But what could she do? She could not go alone back to Sweden and Boppa. Once again, she felt trapped.

That evening Erna, Alfreda, and Mama stayed in the Swedish Travelers' Aid Society lodging. The two-story brick building was sparsely furnished but clean. For dinner they had pea soup with pieces of ham in it—a great luxury back home. They slept in rows of hard beds that squeaked whenever they moved. Mama made sure the America-chest was safe on the floor between their beds before she crawled under her covers and began snoring.

Try as she might, Erna could not sleep. She felt too worried. She did not want to get on another ship. She did not want to be sick the way she had been on the *Tasso*.

Someone else could not sleep. Nearby, two women from Småland whispered in the dark. "I'm not going," one hissed.

"I can't believe how stupid you are," the other replied.

"Something is going to happen. I can feel it."

"You are a fool," her companion replied.

"Nothing is going to happen to you on such a fine, big ship. The *Titanic* cannot sink. That's what the paper said. Go to sleep."

The women kept arguing. Erna listened with half an ear. She wondered if the woman who was afraid would go on the ship. Or would she stay behind? Erna tried hard to hear more, but she was too sleepy to concentrate. After a few moments her eyes closed and she fell sound asleep.

The next day the sky was blue, the sea lazy calm. Erna, Alfreda, and Mama hurried to the dock. It wasn't difficult to find the *Titanic*, the largest steamship in the harbor. The 900-foot long ship rose up nine decks—as tall as an eleven-story building. The great gleaming ship towered over the dock like the side of a cliff. Alfreda and Erna had to tilt their heads backward to see the *Titanic*'s four enormous smokestacks. Unlike the rusty *Tasso*, the *Titanic* was freshly painted. A dazzling gold band of paint encircled the ship's hull or main body.

"Looks like a giant built this boat," Erna said in an awed voice. Boppa had told her many stories of the huge, lumbering supernatural beings that lived on earth before humans.

Mama spit on the ground as an extra precaution against giants' evil. "Must you speak of *jättar* before you sail?" she hissed at Erna. Then, she added in a voice loud enough for any *jättar* who might be hiding nearby to hear, "Giants are stupid creatures, large and strong but easily outsmarted by a clever human. Surely a ship this magnificent was created by someone far more intelligent than a giant."

Alfreda listened to Mama and Erna with annoyance. Would they ever stop their silly clinging to legends and superstitions? "The *Titanic* is completely modern," she told them. "I read in a Swedish advertisement at the White Star Line office that it weighs 46,000 tons. Can you imagine? There are furnaces inside the ship that produce steam with the power of 50,000 horses. That's how the *Titanic* can move."

"Horses?" Mama said, confused. "How can horses swim across the wide ocean pulling a ship so big?"

Alfreda sighed. *Mama will never understand.* "All I'm trying to tell you, Mama, is that it's a steamship. The biggest one ever built. It's completely safe."

"Nothing is completely safe from *sjörå*," Mama murmured.

Alfreda only laughed. "I don't believe in sea

spirits and neither should you. They're ridiculous nonsense."

Mama scowled, then spit. "Don't tempt ill fate!"

Alfreda chuckled. In America, she was certain, no one would worry about *sjörå*, grotesque animallike spirits that hid among rocky dangerous places, played violins, and lured innocent men and women to their deaths in their watery kingdoms. *Sjörå* did not exist except in the wild imaginations of Swedish fishermen who had spent too much time at sea. Everyone knew that.

A strange honking noise filled the air. Erna and her sister watched in amazement as several shining black automobiles pulled up beside the dock. This was the closest either of them had ever been to such amazing machines. Doors swung open and men in proper gray coats and matching caps leaped out and stood in obedient stillness.

Automatically Mama made a low curtsy as if she expected King Oscar to emerge. Mama trembled and seemed unable to look up into the faces of such fine, amazing people. Erna's mouth dropped open as she watched women in fabulous bright hats, carrying bouquets of flowers emerge from the automobiles. They did not even glance at the crowd. Instead, they walked with haughty elegance up the gang plank followed by a retinue of other women not so fancily dressed. A small dog with long, trailing fur barked irritably as it was carried by one of the men in a gray coat.

"Serving girls for those high-class types," Alfreda whispered, "must be paid very well."

Mountains of suitcases and hatboxes and trunks were unloaded from the automobiles. Then more flowers, more gifts wrapped in bright wrappers were heaped up on the dock, awaiting delivery. "Who would have thought we'd be traveling with such fine folk?" Erna whispered.

"I doubt they'll have much to do with the likes of us," Alfreda said in a scoffing voice.

"They're pleasing to look at all the same," Erna replied.

Another loud whistle filled the air. There were no flags waving, no band playing, no speeches. Yet it was clear what was happening. The *Titanic*, dubbed the greatest ship in the world, was starting off on her very first voyage. A small but enthusiastic crowd of citizens from Southampton gathered at the dock to watch the enormous luxury ship venture out into the channel of the River Test.

It was time to say goodbye to Mama.

"We'll all be together again in only a few

weeks," Mama reassured Erna when she began to cry. "You be a good girl and always do what Alfreda says. Remember to be respectful of the authorities. Punishment at sea is swift and terrible. You do not wish to be cast overboard and eaten by fish with sharp teeth, do you?"

Erna shook her head. The idea of leaving Mama behind was nearly as awful as the prospect of hungry fish.

Mama blinked back her own tears, which only made Erna cry harder.

"That's quite enough sobbing, both of you," Alfreda said briskly. *Can't they see how lucky we are to be going?*

Mama tightly embraced Erna. She stroked her youngest daughter's hair. Alfreda worried that Mama might convince Erna to stay behind, thus jeopardizing her own escape. "We'll see you in just a little while, Mama," Alfreda said, prying Erna from her grip. She handed Erna her bundle. Unceremoniously Erna wiped her nose with her sleeve. "We'll be fine," Alfreda insisted.

"You promise you'll take care of Erna?" Mama demanded. "You promise you will always take care of your little sister?"

"Yes, yes, yes," Alfreda said. She hoped she sounded convincing.

"Goodbye, Alfreda," Mama said and hugged her.

Erna embraced her mother one last time. Alfreda took her sister by the arm and began to drag her along the lower gangplank, which was slightly below wharf level. This was the entryway for steerage passengers.

Mama refused to stop giving advice, even as the girls were pushed along by a throng of other third-class passengers. "Don't forget Uncle Frederik will meet you at Ellis Island!" Mama shouted. "He will take you to Papa. Do not go with anyone else. Do not trust anyone else—"

When Erna turned a last time to see Mama, she was too late. Her mother had already been swallowed up by the noisy crowd.

Chapter

6

"Come on!" Alfreda said impatiently. Why couldn't her sister cooperate for once? She tugged Erna by the hand. They had to get on the ship and find their room and put their belongings away. What if someone tried to take their space — two berths in a four-berth cabin at the stern, or the back, of the ship? These accommodations, the agent had told her, were reserved for single women and families traveling together.

"Where are we? Where are we going?" Erna demanded.

Alfreda scowled. "Just follow me." *Why do I have to do all the thinking, all the planning?* Anxiety twisted in the pit of her stomach. Everything had happened so quickly, so perfectly. First the arrival of the tickets sent by Papa and then the availability of berths on the *Titanic*. Even though the train trip from Hull was complicated, they had not become lost once. How long would her good luck hold?

"Can't we stay and wave goodbye?" Erna asked. "Look, we're already pulling away."

"No, the ship's not moving yet," Alfreda said. She looked at the top of the chimneys in the distance. *Maybe Erna's right.* The chimneys seemed to be getting smaller. The *Titanic* was floating away from the quay so slowly and gently, it did not even seem as if they were in motion. *Such a strange enormous ship! Nothing like the* Tasso. "All right. We can wave goodbye, I suppose. No one else seems to be in a hurry to find their rooms just now."

Alfreda and Erna leaned against the railing and watched the fluttering of straw hats and handkerchiefs of people on the dock. Six tugboats escorted the ship, blasting their horns. Suddenly *crack crack crack* rang out. Was it a gun? Nervously Alfreda looked all around. "Did you hear—"

"Look!" Erna said, pointing. Another huge steamship with *New York* painted on one side had broken free from its moorings and was drifting straight into the path of the *Titanic*. Bells clanged aboard the *Titanic*. The girls and the other passengers around them watched in horror as the *New York* swung round. The front of the ship came closer, closer — six feet, five feet, four feet. . . .

Alfreda held her breath. *There goes my luck.*

Erna gripped the hand rail. Suddenly one of the tugboats threw a line across to the *New York*. The little tug puffed and strained, trying to slow down the smaller ship. The waves rose and fell from the enormous *Titanic*, which kept moving forward.

The *New York* swept past with only a few inches to spare as the *Titanic* glided through the narrow channel toward the sea. "That was a close call!" Erna whispered.

Alfreda did not say anything, too fearful that her good fortune might suddenly end.

"I thought you said you wanted to find our room?" Erna asked.

Alfreda nodded. She led her sister along the crowded deck in search of the stairs that would take them below. It was all so confusing. Their ticket said "E37." What did that mean? They tried to stop a steward to ask him, but he couldn't understand what they were saying and simply pointed toward the front of the ship. *What if no one on board speaks Swedish?* A terrible lonely feeling caught in her throat.

Sweating and exhausted, the girls kept moving. They climbed down another set of stairs and soon found their way blocked by a gate and a sign.

"What does it say?" Erna demanded.

Alfreda shrugged. She could not read English words. But clearly it meant for them to go some other way. *What if we never find our room? We might spend the entire voyage walking up and down the corridors.* The *Titanic* seemed as vast as the entire port city of Göteborg. The ship was filled with people who did not speak the same language nor understand anything the girls said. Alfreda and Erna kept descending—one, two, three, four, five sets of steep stairs. Finally they found a steward and showed him their ticket. He motioned for them to follow him. Alfreda felt relieved. *Perhaps now we'll find our way.*

The steward pointed to a door. It was freshly painted and they had to climb over the threshhold to step inside. "No sawdust!" Erna whispered to her sister. The room was small and clean and cold. A set of bunk beds stood on either side of the narrow room. Between the beds against the wall was a small white bowl.

"What's this?" Alfreda asked. She pointed to the bowl. The steward, who seemed eager to leave, impatiently turned something silver and gleaming. Water poured into the bowl. Alfreda gasped. Would the seawater flood in and drown them? He laughed when he saw her terrified expression. With another flick of his wrist, the pouring water ceased.

Curious, Erna reached out to touch the place where the water had vanished.

"Don't!" Alfreda said, worried that they would not be able to stop the water.

The steward chuckled one more time and disappeared out the door.

"Real mattresses! These beds are soft," Erna said. She climbed up the side of the beds, nimble as a squirrel. "No dead bedbugs! And look here—fresh sheets!"

Gingerly Alfreda inspected the bed below her sister's. She looked in all the folds of the sheets and blankets but could not find any dead vermin. "They smell new," she said in wonderment.

Erna flopped down on the bed and gazed up at the ceiling. "This ship does not seem to move and buck like the *Tasso*."

"Do you miss that old tub?" Alfreda asked in a playful voice.

"No!" Erna said and laughed. "This is a wonderful, beautiful ship. It is clean. It is calm." She paused. "I am only worried about one thing."

"What is that?"

Erna pointed to the two empty beds on the other side of the room. "Who will sleep there?"

Alfreda shrugged. "Perhaps the ship's agent did not sell those tickets. We are already on our way, aren't we? And the passengers did not arrive. Perhaps we shall have the room to ourselves."

Erna whistled happily. Perhaps this trip would work out just fine. Contentedly she leaned back with her eyes closed, her fingers laced behind her head. She took a deep breath, entranced by how pleasant everything smelled—even though they were deep inside the ship. *If steerage is this lovely, how grand must first class be?*

"Let's go exploring, Lazy Bones," Alfreda said. She hit her sister with a pillow. "No time for sleeping."

Erna grabbed the pillow and hit her sister in the head. Alfreda laughed and tossed the pillow on the bunk. "Come on!" She dashed out the door with her sister close behind.

Erna could not remember the last time she'd done anything fun with her sister. When Alfreda lived at home, they had worked together, eaten together. But she had few memories of sharing any enjoyable, impractical activities. There never seemed to be time to do anything silly. Besides, her older sister always seemed so serious. When she wasn't doing chores, she had her nose in a book. *But now look at her!* Erna smiled as she watched Alfreda skip down the passageway.

Alfreda ducked inside an open door. Erna followed her. "What's this room?" Erna asked her sister.

"I'm over here!" Alfreda said and laughed.

Erna turned and felt bewildered. *Two Alfredas!* How could her sister be in two places at once? Alfreda raised her hand and smiled. So did her twin. When Erna took a step closer, she could see herself—or a likeness very like herself.

"An enormous mirror—as big as a wall!" the real Alfreda said and laughed. Her reflection laughed, too.

Erna felt her face flush with embarrassment.

"Now, what's over here?" Alfreda poked a door. The door swung open, revealing a white bowl similar to the one that was in their room. Only this one was low to the ground and had another little trapdoor on top. Alfreda lifted the trapdoor. Erna peered over her shoulder. The girls looked at each other in confusion. Alfreda dipped her hand in the water. "Is this for washing clothes?"

Before Erna could answer, a woman came in. She was wearing a uniform. She gave the girls a disdainful look and disappeared inside one of the other doors. Suddenly a loud terrible rush of water was heard. Erna muffled a scream. *Is the sea water coming in again?* She bolted away from the mysterious basin, into the room with mirrors, but she could not find the door. Everything was so confusing.

The woman gave her another withering look as she turned on the metal spigot and water flowed on to her hands. Briskly she shook them dry, then rubbed them with a towel that hung on the wall. She looked at herself critically in the mirror, adjusted a loose shock of hair, and marched out the door.

Alfreda muffled a giggle. "I think I know what this place is."

"What?" Erna demanded.

"It's like the privy back home. Only very fancy. See?" She pointed to the low basin that was filled with water. She pulled on a lever, and the basin made the same noise they had heard before. The water swished around and around and disappeared.

"I'll never use it," Erna said, examining the swirling water nervously.

"Why not?" Alfreda asked.

"Fish from the ocean might swim up and bite me."

Alfreda laughed and laughed. "Erna, you're funny!"

Erna looked at her sister and smiled. *That's the sweetest thing she's ever called me.* She followed her sister out into the hallway. A steward walked past ringing a bell. He called a word over and over. Passengers filed obediently out of their rooms.

"What's he say?" Erna demanded. "Where's everyone going?"

"Let's follow and find out," Alfreda said. The two girls tagged along behind the crowd. They trudged up and down stairs and through long, unfamiliar corridors. Every room looked the same. Alfreda tried hard not to look as worried as she felt. She did not want to frighten her sister. *What if we can never find our way back to our room?*

Somewhere nearby wafted the delicious aroma of fried meat and onions. "I believe we are going to the dining room," Erna whispered. "But they gave us no plates, no silverware. How will we eat?"

Alfreda had no time to think of an answer.

They followed the crowd into the steerage dining room, which was not like any place the girls had ever eaten before in their lives. For a moment they could not think what to say, what to do. They gawked at the long, gleaming white tables and the glittering, sturdy white dishes and forks and knives and cups set out as if awaiting honored guests. "No sawdust," Erna whispered and pointed. "No greasy sign on the wall."

The girls watched the other passengers take their seats on benches that lined each long table. Alfreda and Erna did the same. People in white coats carried in platters heaped with potatoes and meat and something green that Alfreda did not recognize. They passed these to each passenger. In the middle of each table the white-coats placed plates heaped with white bread soft as cake and big tubs of fresh butter. People helped themselves to as much as they wanted.

Erna and her sister ate greedily before the white-coats could notice that they had been given too much. Erna slipped pieces of bread inside her pocket and motioned for seconds of glasses of sweet, lemon-flavored water. Everything was available in such abundance that Alfreda felt suspicious. But she felt glad to see her skinny sister eating her fill. She winked at Erna. *Perhaps she'll plump out a bit.*

"This your first trip on a steamship?" a blond girl wearing thick glasses said in Swedish. She smiled at Alfreda. "You can ask for more meat if you wish. My name is Elin. This is my friend Berta. She knows English perfectly."

Berta, who sat beside Alfreda, kept chewing and did not speak. She was a heavyset girl with dark hair and blue eyes. Her hair was combed straight up like the young women in one of the America-pictures. Alfreda wondered what she was doing on the ship.

Alfreda introduced herself and said, "This is my sister, Erna."

Erna bobbed her head shyly and took a sip of the lemon water.

Berta cleared her throat. She dabbed at the corners of her mouth with a white napkin. "When we dock at Cherbourg, you must hurry to your room and lock your door."

"Why?" Alfreda asked nervously.

"Because there are dirty foreigners coming aboard. Frenchmen and Poles and Arabs. Maybe some Chinese," Berta said with authority. "They will take the empty beds in your cabin. They will cook their own smelly food and fill your berths with terrible odors. And they will steal from you while you are asleep."

"How do you know this?" Alfreda asked.

Elin smiled with admiration at her traveling companion. "Berta has taken this trip before across the ocean. She is returning to America from spending some time in Sweden visiting her family."

Berta nodded wisely. "I know everything about America. I know everything about steamships. When we dock in Queenstown tomorrow, the Irish will come aboard. They are the worst of all."

Alfreda remembered the smelly old woman aboard the *Tasso*. *What should we do? Lock the door?*

Berta smiled confidingly. "All you need to do is keep the door shut and shout these English words: '*I am very ill. I vomit on floor.*' Then they'll go away and find another room."

"'*I ham ferry ill. I fomit on floor,*'" Alfreda repeated.

Elin giggled. Alfreda blushed. Had she said the mysterious phrase wrong?

"Good job," Berta said. "You will learn English quickly once you reach America."

Alfreda could not help feeling disappointed. "I must learn the language right away," she said quietly. "I cannot wait until then. Please tell me. What is it like in America?"

Berta was silent for several moments. "America is very different from Sweden. There are people with black skin there."

"Black skin?" Erna said, surprised. "How can that be?"

Berta shrugged. "That is the way they are. There are people with brown skin, too. They are called Indians."

"*Indians,*" Alfreda said, rolling this word over and over in her mouth. "And are there many white people, too? People who look like us?"

"They look like us but they do not speak like us or eat like us or dress like us. Some come from many different places, many different countries."

This was a situation that Alfreda could hardly imagine. In Sweden everyone had the same skin color. "And do they get along?"

"Most of the time," Berta said and smiled. "You will be too busy working to worry about that. In America you will work very hard."

"Oh, I am not afraid to work. I have worked hard all my life," Alfreda said. "But what can you tell me about the schools in America? Are they very costly?"

"In some places you may pay the teacher a few

dollars each month to go to school. Anyone can go to school."

"Anyone?"

Berta nodded.

This was the best news of all! Alfreda licked her lips. She would learn English and she would go to school in America. A few dollars wasn't very much. Why, she would be making so much money, she might even buy a new purse to carry to school. She would buy books, too. She could hardly wait. "Berta, thank you for your advice. Now if you'll please excuse us? We want to make sure no foreigner moves into our room," Alfreda said, signaling to her sister. *What luck to have met such a helpful traveler!*

Chapter 7

Alfreda and Erna tried to retrace their way back to their room, but became hopelessly lost. "What's that crying sound?" Erna asked. She crept along the corridor. There was a loud booming of a machine, but higher up, like the shrill whine of someone crying. It sounded like a young child. *Perhaps it's a baby kidnapped by a troll!* Such things happened all the time back home. In Erna's village they called troll kidnappings *bertagning*, "to be taken into the mountain."

"Where do you think you're going?" Alfreda demanded.

Erna paid no attention to her sister. She pushed open a door. Steam and cooking smells enveloped her. She could see a great vat of water and hear the clinking of dishes and the sound of laughter. The crying noise was getting louder. Noiselessly and stealthily she crept along. There was a poor child trapped in this evil troll place. She felt sure of it.

"Come back here!" Alfreda called to her.

Erna tiptoed noiselessly along. Her heart pounded. She was on a rescue mission. Nothing could stop her. She ducked low and followed a row of shelves and doors. The crying sound became louder now. She looked inside the dark opening. Shining eyes stared out at her! She muffled a scream.

But neither or troll nor a baby glared out at her. *Cat's eyes!* A swarm of kittens each no bigger than her hand swarmed around a larger black-and-white cat that looked out at her and blinked.

Erna gulped. "Hello, Kitty!" she said, relieved not to find a troll. She pulled out a piece of bread from her pocket and tore it into smaller chunks for the mother cat. The little black-and-white kittens were still blind. Their eyes were shut. They were not interested in bread.

A man's questioning voice boomed overhead.

Erna looked up, terrified. The man's scowling face was red—even his bald scalp was red. *What did he say?* He folded his hairy, scalded-looking arms over his enormous white apron. *What should I do?* Trembling, she held up the piece of bread. Then she pointed to the cat—as if to show she didn't mean any harm. She only meant to offer food to the cats.

When the man saw what she was doing, his expression changed. He smiled. He pointed to the mother cat and said one word: "Jenny."

"Yenny," Erna repeated.

"Jenny," the man said again.

"Jenny." Erna grinned. She had just spoken her first English word in front of an English person. She felt very bold.

"Come on!" Alfreda hissed. She grabbed Erna by the arm. She tried to apologize to the big white-aproned man in Swedish. When the man did not understand, she blurted the first English phrase she had learned from her English phrase book. She was so scared, she couldn't remember what it meant. *" 'Ti and biskits,' "* she said. *" 'Ti and biskits.' "*

The man roared with laughter. He pointed to the doorway. Humiliated, Alfreda pulled her sister along so that they could make their escape. "Don't ever run away like that again," Alfreda whispered as they headed down the corridor again. "Mama said I'm to look after you. How can I do that when you purposefully disappear?"

"I won't disappear again," Erna promised. Secretly she felt pleased by her sister's distress. *Maybe she likes me after all.* "Would you like to hear the new English word I just learned?"

Alfreda nodded.

"Jenny."

Alfreda looked confused. "What does it mean?"

"It means cat," Erna said proudly.

❧

April 10, 1912

Dearest Always-remembered Boppa:

I come to you with a few lines. Let you know that I am well in body and the same gift of the good Lord I wisht for you. We are aboard the *Titanic,* which is the biggest ship in the world and much confusion for someone as small as me. But we find our way. Alfreda is a dear sister after all and she helps me as a mother might which gives me great pleasure because I am not lonely or sad as I might be if I were traveling across the wide ocean by myself. Sometimes she is bossy, which makes me angry. She can lack patience but most often she is very happy I think because she leaves Sweden. Someone told us there is a big tank for bathing and a steam room and a room with pretend horses for the rich folk to ride. I cannot imagine such things. Do you suppose someone tells us this to fool us? We are not so stupid. We have had some adventures already. When the passengers came on from Cherbourg—what a great noise and shouts and pushing! Mobs of people speaking all kinds of tongues I did not know. Babies screaming. Fathers and mothers searching for lost childrens. Much arguing, waving arms. Alfreda and I dashed to our room and slammed the door because we did not want to share our space with someone who might rob us while we slept. Someone came and knocked loud and shouted. Alfreda knows a little English now. She and I leaned hard on the door to keep it shut. She called *"I ham ferry ill. I fomit on floor."* So the family left and found some other place. Is my sister not clever? I saw some of these girls from faraway places called Pole Land and France. They wear kerchiefs on their heads like us but no wood shoes. Some are very dirty, the babies especially. The girls my age are frightened as deer in the woods. Boppa, I miss you vary much. I miss trees. Everything is new and full of wind. I pray we get to safety to dry land in New York soon. Alfreda sends greetings. Hello to Grandmother. I must mail this before we reach Queenstown.

> Your fond granddaughter,
> Erna

P.S. I found a cat that just had kittens. Alfreda won't let me ask to keep one. She says they are to catch mice. I haven't seen one mouse on this fine ship.

❧

The next day Alfreda and Erna sat on the steerage promenade deck at the very back of the boat, a place Alfreda had learned was officially called the stern. "The front of the ship is called the bow," Alfreda said with authority.

"Oh," said Erna, unimpressed.

Out on the open deck there was plenty of space to sit and enjoy the sunlight and the bright blue sky and listen to the drumming lullaby hum of the propellers that churned underwater deep below. When Erna looked backward at the way they had come, she saw that the ship had made a long snaky white path. Birds followed them, crying in loud, sad voices. Erna could watch the birds for hours.

Even though the weather was so fine, Alfreda said they must work on their English lesson. She read aloud from *The Emigrant's Interpreter* in a very important voice, which Erna found irritating. She'd rather go exploring or bounce the little ball that Elin and Berta had bought. "When we are finished, you can play," Alfreda said, as if she were already a teacher. "Repeat after me:

"Vatt land is itt vi si thar?"

Erna did as she was told. She stumbled through the words, even though she did not know exactly what they meant.

Alfreda continued, *"It is neufaundland. Vi are suhn arrived—"*

"Look at those elegant ladies!" Erna interrupted. She pointed to the first-class passengers who looked down on them from a deck several stories above the steerage deck. The women had to hold on to their huge purple hats to keep them from blowing away.

Alfreda rapped her finger against the wooden deck floor. "Please pay attention and repeat what I say: *"Vhatt a bejuitufll prospact!"*

Erna sighed and said the words.

"Nau ju ma gaa ann chorr."

"Vatt du ju cahl this place?"
"Itt is cahled Ellis Island."

Secretly Erna thought she'd never understand English. But she did not want to disappoint her sister, who seemed so determined to master the language before they stepped foot in America. "Can we go look around now?" Erna begged.

Alfreda shut the book. "I suppose."

The girls climbed down the stairs. "I have heard there is something called the Third-Class Smoking Room below us," Alfreda said. "Follow me."

"Are you sure we are allowed in such a place?" Erna asked. She saw a door made of glass and beyond was the sound of men's laughter and the clinking of glasses. Someone was playing a piano. She pushed open the door so that they could both peek inside. "It seems awfully fancy, doesn't it?"

"I see no gates barring our way," Alfreda replied. She walked in, head high, practicing the manner in which she would walk when she came to America, where everyone was equal and there was liberty and justice for all.

The young men gathered around the piano hooted loudly when they saw Alfreda and Erna. The girls paused. "Let's go back," Erna hissed. There were no other women or girls to be seen anywhere in this fine room. "Maybe we're not allowed."

Alfreda ignored her. She kept walking.

She's too tough, too bold for her own good. Erna bit her lip nervously, but shadowed her sister into the room.

A surly man in a white coat leaned against the wall with a dirty towel over his arm. When he saw the girls, he flapped the towel in their direction and said something in an angry voice. He pointed at the door. There was a sign in English.

What does it say? Desperately Erna tugged on her sister's arm. "Let's get out of here before we get into trouble. Come along! Don't be a pushy piece of string."

Alfreda gave up in her stubborn demonstration of their rights. She turned and followed Erna out the door. The steward followed them a few feet. He disdainfully snapped his towel after them as if they were nothing more than two stray flies trying to land in newly churned milk.

Erna made a buzzing noise. Alfreda grinned. Soon they were both giggling and bumbling down the corridor pretending to be flies.

"What did you mean by a pushy piece of string?" Alfreda demanded, out of breath. She and Erna leaned against the stairway wall.

"It's an old, old story Boppa once told me," Erna said.

"Tell it." Alfreda sat on the step and held her knees in her arms.

"Some people were out in the fields bringing in the hay," Erna said. "They'd brought along a little boy and left him by himself at the edge of the field with a jar of milk with some pieces of bread in it. He sat there eating with a spoon when along came a snake—something the little boy had never seen before."

"Was it a dangerous snake?" Alfreda demanded.

Erna rubbed her forehead. "Let me tell what happens next."

"Wasn't the little one afraid?"

"Please don't interrupt," Erna said. Now she knew what it felt like when her sister tried to tell her something important and she wouldn't listen. "Where was I? Oh, yes. This snake poked his snout into the jar and started greedily drinking the milk. *Gulp-gulp-gulp*. For a while the little boy sat watching while the snake drank. But then he hit him on the head with the spoon saying, 'You've got to eat the bread, too, you pushy piece of string.' "

Alfreda laughed. "Am I a pushy piece of string?"

"Sometimes you are nearly as demanding as that snake," Erna said, giggling. She felt surprised that she could say these words to her sister and not worry her sister would be angry.

Alfreda stood up and brushed off the back of her dress. She watched her sister hopping from one step to another. She had never noticed that her little sister could be so amusing. *Erna makes me laugh.*

The regular humming noise that surged through the ship suddenly changed. Erna and Alfreda could feel the difference in the soles of their feet. The floor wasn't vibrating the way it had before. What was happening? The girls hurried up on deck just in time to see a red-and-white flag hoisted high overhead.

"What's that for?" Erna asked.

Alfreda shrugged. In the distance they could see land. They seemed to be coming into another harbor. The *Titanic* stopped. "I spot another boat. One with oars. It's still a ways off," said Alfreda. "How will they ever get on board?"

The girls and the other people from steerage leaned out over the edge to watch as an incredibly long rope ladder was lowered and a man no bigger than an ant began to climb his perilous way up the ladder. After another long wait, the *Titanic* began moving again, closer to land.

"Queenstown," announced Berta, who joined Alfreda and Erna. Elin stood beside her. "Another pilot came aboard to show our captain the way into Cork Harbor, where we'll be anchored."

From one of the docks along the harbor came two smaller ships that Berta called "tenders." These boats, painted with the names *Ireland* and *America*, looked crowded with passengers and bulky canvas bags. The transfer of people and baggage seemed to take forever. Everyone in steerage watched the activity.

Suddenly a shout rang out. A man waved his arm in the air and pointed with one finger at one of the four enormous *Titanic* smokestacks. A woman screamed. Alfreda and Erna looked up and saw a black-faced figure sticking out of the very top of the smokestack. The figure waved. "A troll!" Erna whispered in terror. She clamped her hands over her eyes.

"A devil," Elin said fearfully.

"It's only a joke," Berta replied with a chuckle. "Can't you see? I bet it was one of the stokers who climbed up the smokestack just to show off."

"What's a stoker?" Alfreda demanded in a quavering voice.

"One of the fellows who shovels coal into the great furnaces below. That's what drives the engines that move this ship," Berta said importantly. Other Swedish passengers gathered around her and listened. "Stokers' faces are always blackened with soot."

"I think it's a bad omen all the same," Elin said darkly. "How did he get up there? Why wasn't he burned? Only the devil could withstand such heat."

For several moments no one said anything. They just stood and looked up, as if trying to make sense of what had happened. As quickly as the face appeared, it disappeared. Without warning, the *Titanic* gave three long blasts on her siren. The two tenders echoed the call. Then the *Titanic* made one last lonesome toot. The tenders answered—a final howling farewell.

"I forgot!" Alfreda said, giving her sister a frantic shove. "The Irish!"

Obediently Erna followed her sister down the steps, through the winding corridor to their room. But they were too late. Erna and Alfreda tried to push the door open. It would not budge. They could hear cackling laughter on the other side. Alfreda banged hard and shouted. Erna shouldered the door with all her might. Finally a pale face peeked through the crack. One bright blue eye. A high-pitched, singsong voice spoke. Neither Alfreda nor her sister could understand a word the Irish girl was saying.

Desperately Alfreda took a running start and threw herself against the door. At the last moment the door swung open. Alfreda tumbled in and fell on the floor. Her wooden shoes fell off her feet, and the holes in her stocking feet showed. She sat up, blushing angrily.

"Are you all right?" Erna asked. Fearfully she looked over her shoulder at the rude Irish girls who obviously thought the scene very amusing.

"I'm fine," Alfreda said. She stood up and gave the two Irish girls angry scowls. The two girls made faces back and laughed heartily. Alfreda pushed up her sleeves. *I'll box your ears.*

As if sensing danger, the girl with the fair hair jumped quickly up on the top bunk and stuck out her tongue.

"Get out!" Alfreda shouted. She pointed toward the door. She picked up one of the girl's shabby valises and tossed it into the hallway. In a flash the girl was off the bed and dashed into the corridor to retrieve her belongings. Alfreda slammed the door shut. When she turned, she realized she had inadvertently allowed the other Irish girl to remain.

"Help!" shouted Erna, who struggled to keep the captive from tearing up their bedding.

The Irish girl who had been locked out began banging loudly on the door. But Alfreda felt determined to keep her outside. *I'll stay here the rest of the voyage to bar her way back in.*

Suddenly a man hollered from the other side of the door. He called in an authoritative manner that convinced Alfreda to open the door. It was the steward. He looked angry. He said something in English. He picked up the Irish girl who had been stranded in the hallway and roughly shoved her into the room. Then he dusted off his hands and marched away.

The Irish girls waited until his footsteps disappeared before they both repeated a word that sounded to Alfreda like some kind of hissing insult. Out of breath and exhausted, the Irish girls and Alfreda and her sister retreated to their own beds. Alfreda still felt very angry. She glowered at the smiling face that popped into view. It was the Irish girl with fair hair. She seemed rather fancy, Alfreda thought. On one finger she wore a gold ring, and she had a lace collar. *Who would think someone like this could be such a good fighter?*

The dark-haired Irish girl used sign language. She pointed to Alfreda's arm and nodded, as if admiring her strength. She grinned. Then she pointed to herself and said, "Nora Hagarty." She motioned toward her companion. "Bridget O'Neill."

Erna watched all this and felt as if she were observing the passing of a sudden summer rainstorm. They weren't fighting, but they weren't friends exactly. It seemed to her to be an uneasy peace. She slipped her hand under her pillow to make sure the *tomte* was all right. The little statue looked at her with his wry, silly smile, and she wondered what Boppa would make of all that had happened to them.

A loud gong was heard in the hallway. Alfreda and Erna scrambled from their beds and headed down toward the third-class dining room. Alfreda seemed especially eager to escape from their new Irish roommates. "Can you believe those barbarians?" Alfreda said. She hurried quickly and did not look back to see if Nora and Bridget were following them. Once in the dining room they found seats with Elin and Berta.

In great detail Alfreda told the Swedish girls of the arrival of the terrible injustices they had suffered at the hands of these Irish foreigners. Elin and Berta nodded sympathetically. "It's too bad everyone on the ship isn't Swedish," Elin said in a low voice.

"Things would be much better," Berta agreed. "Imagine our shock today when we spied some Chinese men wearing their hair in single pigtails. Have you ever heard of anything so odd?" She laughed. So did Elin and Alfreda.

Only Erna was quiet. She did not think her sister had told the whole truth. *She behaved as rudely to them as they did to her.* Erna ate her boiled meat and boiled cabbage without much enthusiasm.

Chapter

8

When dinner ended, Erna followed her sister the long way through the winding corridors and up and down steps to the deck. Countless stars studded the sky. The air felt cold and biting. "I wish our trip would never end," Alfreda announced. She gazed heavenward and held her elbows tight against herself.

Erna felt uneasy. She looked out into the dark sea and thought of evil ocean sprites. What if one of them heard what her sister said? "You should be careful to say such things in front of *sjörå,*" Erna whispered.

"Don't be silly!" Alfreda replied, laughing. "When you get to America, you will forget everything about *sjörå* and the Old Country."

Forget everything? Somehow this idea only made Erna feel sad.

"You're so quiet. Is something wrong?" Alfreda asked.

Erna took a deep breath. "How will we recognize Papa? I cannot remember what he looks like. Do you?"

"We have seen his America-picture."

Erna remained silent. *What if he's changed?*

"I was older than you when he left. I will know him when I see him," Alfreda said confidently. "Do you hear music?"

Erna listened. It wasn't *sjörå*. The sounds of violins came from somewhere below them—inside the ship. Someone was singing. The girls crept down the stairs and peeked into the Smoking Room. This time there was no steward flapping a towel at them inside the door. And in the room were women dancing. Girls no older than Alfreda were twirling arm in arm with young men. It was hot and crowded and smoky, but everyone seemed to be enjoying themselves. Now a wild dancing melody rocked the room. Even though most people could not understand each other's languages, they seemed to understand the music.

A young blond boy chased another boy in wooden shoes. They laughed and called to each other. Erna suddenly took a deep breath. *Karl!* Was it possible? She crept closer, half convincing herself that the skinny boy was her brother. When he turned, she could see it was not Karl.

"Mama!" the boy cried and ran away from her.

Strange, new music filled the room. A man held a set of strange pipes and a soft bag under one arm. He pressed the bag with his arm. The sound reminded Erna of the howling wind. The lively music swept the dancers into the cleared area of the room. A freckled boy no taller than Alfreda made a curt bow and offered her his arm. Instead of punching him, she linked arms and went dancing away. Erna watched in amazement. *What a contradiction Alfreda is!* One minute serious, the next full of tricks. One minute angry, the next laughing.

Elin and Berta sailed past, kicking up their heels and laughing. They had slipped off their wooden shoes and were dancing in their stocking feet. They motioned for Erna to join them. In less than a second, Erna had kicked off her shoes, too, and was dancing in a circle round and round until she was dizzy. For the first time she, too, wished that the voyage would never end.

At ten o'clock another bell sounded to indicate that it was time for everyone in steerage to head back to their berths. Some people who were dancing stopped and left willingly. Others motioned to the violinist and piper, indicating that the party would continue elsewhere on the ship. Exhausted but happy, Erna followed her sister back to their room. She was glad that neither Nora nor Bridget was there.

"Good night!" Erna said to her sister and climbed into her bed.

"Good night!" Alfreda replied. "Did you say your prayers?"

Erna said them quickly to herself, then tucked the *tomte* under her pillow so that she would have good dreams. In a moment she was sound asleep.

In the middle of the night, there was a terrible crashing and hollering in the hallway. The door swung open. Alfreda sat up. "Who is it?" she asked fearfully.

Bridget and Nora clambered noisily into their beds. They laughed and shushed each other. Alfreda heard them climb into their beds and collapse with thuds on their mattresses. After a few moments they began snoring.

Now how can I sleep? Alfreda felt angry to have been awakened. At least they did not wake Erna. Erna could sleep through anything. As Alfreda lay in bed, she concentrated on the steady drumming sound of the motor and the propellers. It reminded her of the surf along the rocky coast in Alna. She smiled in the dark, glad not to be sleeping in her aunt and uncle's drafty kitchen. She was on her way to freedom in America.

Later, everyone was still sleeping, Erna awoke from a terrible dream. She sat upright in the dark, her heart pounding. *The kittens!* In her nightmare, the kittens were calling to her from the privy. They were in the swirling water, but when she tried to save them, she couldn't move her legs. She could do nothing . . .

Erna rubbed her eyes, afraid to go back to sleep. *What if the dream returns?* She listened. She could hear Alfreda snoring. Silently she slipped her feet out from under the blanket and lowered herself to the floor. Her legs seemed to be working all right. *Thank goodness!* The floor felt cold even through her socks. She bent over and picked up her wooden clogs, opened the door as quietly as she could, and crept out into the corridor. No one else seemed to be awake.

There were no windows, so she couldn't tell if it was still nighttime or very early morning. Was the weather outside stormy or calm? The ship did not rock or pitch, so she could only assume there was no wind. She had to hurry before Alfreda woke up and found out she was gone. There wasn't a moment to lose.

She hurried along the corridor and sniffed. Cigarette smoke. Sometimes she'd noticed the stewards puffing away when they thought no one important was watching. What if a steward saw her and asked what *she* was doing? Erna walked faster. She saw a door that was open a few inches. From the other side came the sound of joking voices, splashing water, and the metallic sound of pots and pans clanging.

This is the place.

She pushed the door open. The smell of fried meat and potatoes made her stomach growl. Was the bald man with the apron busy washing dishes? Stealthily she crept into the kitchen. She pushed open the low cupboard door, holding her breath. She felt relieved to see a furry black face staring up at her. The big mother cat stretched and yawned as if to say, "Where have you been?" The eight black-and-white kittens lay in a sweet-smelling, cozy heap. The mother cat stood up, stepped out of the cupboard, shook once, and left.

"Where are you going?" Erna whispered. *What if she doesn't come back?* The kittens seemed unconcerned. They kept sleeping. *One-two-three-four-five-*

six. That was a lot of babies to keep track of all at once.

Erna leaned over and picked up the fattest kitten, who lay rudely with its front paws covering the face of a smaller sister. The kitten was no bigger than a mouse. She held the kitten tenderly in her two cupped hands. The soft, warm kitten's heart drummed against her thumb. She stared at its face, its big eyes still closed tight. Everything about it was in miniature. Tiny feet, tiny nose, tiny tail. She stroked its sleek black head and admired its fur. She wished she could keep this kitten. It could sleep on her bed. She could give it scraps of food. Boppa's *tomte* was a great treasure, but it could not move, it was not alive. Not like this kitten—

"Hello, Tea and Biscuits!" a voice barked.

Terrified, Erna looked up. The bald man with the apron loomed above her, his head curiously cocked to one side. Erna lifted the little kitten and spoke the only English word she knew: *"Jenny."*

The man smiled. He wiped his enormous hands on his apron, then he bent over and peered into the cupboard. But he did not seem disturbed that the mother cat had vanished. He leaned back against the wall and rubbed the back of his neck as if he were very tired.

Erna watched him. She wished she could say something to him. She wished he could understand her. Since they could not speak, she held the plump, dozing kitten in her lap and petted it. The man watched her and looked pleased. He stepped away from the wall and shouted something to someone else in the kitchen. Erna froze, terrified that he might be telling someone she'd trespassed into the kitchen. When nothing happened and no one rushed to throw her out, she relaxed. She tried hard to hear what he was saying to the other kitchen worker. Something about the music of his words reminded her of the way Bridget and Nora spoke.

When he reappeared, he carried a fork and a plate heaped with fried potatoes and meat and a cooked egg. He handed her the plate and smiled. At that moment she felt as if they spoke the same language. *He knows I'm hungry.* Carefully she replaced the kitten in the cupboard. She ate her breakfast cross-legged on the floor. The potatoes were crisply fried and the pork tasted tender. She ate every speck.

"*Sverige?*" the man asked, taking the plate from her.

Erna nodded. He knew how to say where she was from. Sweden.

"Ireland," the man replied, pointing to himself.

She did not know that word, but thought perhaps it referred to his country, too.

He reached into his pocket and produced a folded piece of leather. From inside the leather, he proudly removed a small photograph. He handed this to Erna. She looked at it carefully. The photograph was of a young girl, no older than herself. She wore a white pinafore and a white bow in her dark curly hair. She leaned forward slightly. The girl had the same dimples, the same smile as the bald man with the apron. *This must be his daughter.*

For some odd reason, she thought of Papa. What had Boppa told her about her father when she left? *"He loves you, too."* She knew Papa owned no precious photograph of her or her sister to show strangers. Mama said such pictures were too costly. Erna stared at the girl in the photo. Did Papa miss her and her sister the same way this man seemed to miss his little girl?

She handed back the photograph. The man tucked it inside his wallet. Then she had a terrible thought. *What if Papa doesn't recognize me and Alfreda?*

Alfreda! She had almost completely forgotten. Her sister might be awake by now. *She'll be frantic with worry.* Erna leapt to her feet. She hurriedly thanked the man with the apron again and rushed back into the corridor. She ran as fast as she could back to their berth and opened the door. The room was still dark as she jumped into bed.

"What are you doing?" Alfreda asked sleepily.

"Nothing." Erna smiled to herself and closed her eyes.

Later that morning Erna and Alfreda sat on the steerage deck. The weather was clear and sunny. While Alfreda scribbled something, Erna studied the fine first-class passengers who strolled about on the distant promenade. The first-class passengers could look down on the steerage passengers because their special deck was higher.

The ladies' long skirts billowed in the wind. Some carried parasols to shield them from the sunshine. Others seemed to be eating something. A tiny-looking boy in short pants and a cap spun a top on the deck. As Erna watched, she wondered if she should tell Alfreda about her visit to the kittens earlier that morning. Somehow she felt delightfully powerful keeping the visit a secret from her know-it-all sister.

"What are you doing?" Erna asked Alfreda.

"Writing a postcard to Maria Charlotta," Alfreda said. "I'll read it to you if you like." She cleared her throat and read:

❧

"Dear Maria Charlotta in Chicago, U.S.A.:
We are floating along on a beautiful, big boat. Haven't been seasick once. Food is good and plentiful. Am anxious to see America. Your friend, Alfreda."

❧

Erna frowned. "That's not much."

"A postcard doesn't leave a lot of room," Alfreda explained. She showed Erna the colorful photograph of the *Titanic.* On the reverse side was a small white space where she had carefully penned her message.

Erna thought writing on such a lovely photo was a terrible waste. Back home anything as lovely as this postcard would be placed in the parlor. But on their way to America such expensive pictures were simply scribbled on. *How will I ever understand everything I need to know about America?*

"Look at them!" Alfreda said, nudging Erna.

Nora and Bridget stood at the edge of the deck as close as possible to the distant ladies' view. They waved and called to the first-class passengers. A gentleman joined the ladies. He lifted one hand as if to salute Nora and Bridget. Immediately the Irish girls began to sing. They linked arms and rocked back and forth as they loudly sang a haunting melody. Though neither Erna nor Alfreda could understand the words, they listened carefully to the girls' lovely voices. Everyone on the steerage deck listened, too. When Nora and Bridget finished singing, they bowed. The ladies and gentleman in faraway first-class clapped. Although they were too far away for their applause to be heard, Erna could see that they were impressed.

Bridget and Nora called out something to the first-class audience. The ladies and gentleman threw down candy wrapped in bright papers. The Irish girls scrambled to gather up the sweets before the other children in steerage could grab them. They scooped them up into their skirts as the ladies and gentleman laughed and pointed.

"Lucky!" Erna cried and clapped. She could not believe how generous the first-class passengers were to share their candy.

Alfreda frowned. "It's no great sacrifice to give away a few treats like that," she said. *When I get to America I will not have to grovel like some trained animal for rich people. I will be their equal.*

"What's going on here?" Elin asked. She and Berta sat down beside Alfreda and her sister.

Before Alfreda could answer, Bridget approached. Her face was flushed and she was smiling. Her skirt was filled with gold and silver foil-wrapped candies. She said something and dumped the contents of her skirt into Alfreda's lap.

Speechless but suspicious, Alfreda stared at the candy.

Berta nudged Alfreda. "She says, 'The treats are for you. For disturbing your sleep.' What's that supposed to mean?"

"Thank you very much," Alfreda said in her best English. For the first time, she smiled at Bridget and Nora. And they smiled back.

Erna eagerly grabbed a handful of candy. She untwisted the foil and popped the bright red candy in her mouth. *Strawberry!* "Try one, Berta. They're delicious."

Berta shook her head. She scowled at the Irish girls as they wandered to the other side of the deck. "I wouldn't trust them if I were you," she said in a low voice. "They're Irish, you know."

"Well, their candy tastes all right," Erna insisted.

"You Swedes from the Old Country are so gullible," Berta said in a superior voice. "You believe anything. Did you ever hear the story about the old *Svensk* father and the telegraph wires?"

"Tell it! Oh, it's a good one. You'll see," Elin said and nudged Alfreda knowingly with her elbow.

Erna noisily sucked the candy and did not say anything. She wanted to hear the amusing story, even though she had a feeling Berta and Elin were making fun of her and her sister.

"Once a boy wrote home from America that he had bad boots," Berta said. "The father wanted to send him a pair of new ones, but since he'd heard that the telegraph was much faster than the mails, he threw the boots up onto the telegraph wires so that they would get to America quickly."

Elin giggled. Erna could not see what was so funny. "What's a telegraph wire?"

Elin burst into a loud chuckle. "You *are* a country bumpkin! A telegraph wire is a long cable held up in the air by tall poles. Messages are sent on this wire from city to city."

Alfreda's face reddened with embarrassment. Her sister was so stupid!

"Let me finish the story," Berta said. "Before long, a tramp came by, and when he noticed the splendid new boots, he pulled them down and threw his old, worn-out boots up there instead. When the old man saw the worn-out boots a little while later, he believed that the son had gotten the new ones and sent the old ones home!"

Elin hooted with laughter. She laughed and laughed. So did Berta and Alfreda. They slapped each other on the back. Tears ran down their faces. But Erna did not think the story was very funny. The good-hearted old man reminded her of Boppa. *He probably made a great sacrifice to pay for such expensive boots for his son.* Thinking of Boppa made Erna feel homesick. She turned away from her laughing sister and her friends and looked east, the way they'd come. At that moment Sweden seemed farther away than ever.

Chapter

9

As the girls sat on the deck, one of the women stewards bustled into view. She carried a clipboard. She held a long tube to her mouth that made her voice very loud as she marched among the other steerage passengers, who huddled in frightened groups.

"What's she saying?" Alfreda asked Berta.

"Tell us," Elin demanded. "I hope it's nothing serious."

Berta made a face. "Lice have been discovered among some steerage passengers."

"Lice?" Alfreda said, aghast. Instinctively her hand went to her hair. How could there be lice on such a perfect, modern boat as the *Titanic?* To make matters worse, they had left the special fine-toothed comb and salve that Grandmother had packed for them in the big America-chest with Mama.

"The stewardess says everyone must take baths," Berta said, "so that the pestilence is eliminated before it reaches first class."

"I won't take a bath. Baths are not healthy," Erna insisted. "No one takes a bath at home."

"You won't have any choice," Elin said in a mocking voice. "Now that you are going to America, you must give up your Old Country ways."

Alfreda frowned. *Maybe the Irish started the spread of lice.* She scratched her head. She should never have accepted their candy. "Stop whining, Erna," Alfreda said. Must her sister's backwardness humiliate her *again* in front of modern, American Berta?

"The bath won't be so bad, I'm sure," Elin told Erna as the girls filed back to their rooms to await instructions.

After a long wait the women and girls in their corridor of the ship lined up to take a bath in the echoing, tiled room with a big metal tub. Erna felt very frightened when it was her turn. She did not wish to give up her clothing and stand shivering and naked. She did not like the unpleasant glance the bath attendant gave her when she poured something green into the water. The spicy smell of the green water made Erna sneeze.

As soon as the bath attendant turned her back, Erna dropped her towel and quickly stepped into the warm tub. She sat down. The bath attendant dumped a bucket of green water on her head. This was such a shock that Erna choked and gasped. She couldn't breathe. She couldn't see. She rubbed her eyes just as the bath attendant dumped another green bucket of water on her head. Erna sputtered indignantly. She thought she might start to cry any moment. *How long can this torture go on?*

Suddenly the bath steward tossed a towel on the side of the tub and disappeared. Erna's teeth chattered. She knew she had to get out now and dry herself. What if the woman had burned her clothing? She had heard that was one way to get rid of lice. She owned only one other dress. It was unfair, really, to have her clothing destroyed.

Erna pulled herself to her feet and was about to step out of the tub, when she felt something under her heel. She reached under the water. The object at the bottom of the tub seemed to be round and hard, almost like a coin. She picked it up.

A gold ring!

The bath attendant bustled into the room and motioned for her to hurry. Erna gripped the ring tightly between her fingers so that it would not fall back into the water again. She stepped out of the tub, dried herself, and padded into the adjoining room where Alfreda was waiting for her.

"What took you so long?" Alfreda whispered. She was wrapped in a towel. Her teeth chattered and her lips were nearly blue.

Erna glanced over her shoulder to make sure no one was watching. "Look what I found in the tub." She showed her sister the gold ring.

Alfreda examined the ring carefully. The plain gold band shimmered. She held it up to the light to see if there were any special markings. Perhaps on the inside of the ring. "Strange," she said in a low voice.

"What?" Erna demanded.

"There seems to be a name engraved inside. See?"

"Maybe it's the owner."

Alfreda stared hard at the two words. They weren't Swedish. As best she could, she sounded them out: " 'Sinn Fein.' "

At that moment, the bath attendant bustled into the room. When she heard Alfreda say these words, she turned pale. She rushed to Alfreda and grabbed her by the arm. Her face looked frightened and angry at the same time.

Instinctively Alfreda tried to hide the ring. But the bath attendant pried it out of her fingers. The woman's hands shook as she read the inscription for herself. She pushed Alfreda and her sister into the changing area and pointed to their clothing, which was now covered with a fine, white dust that had a strange peppery odor.

The bath attendant stepped outside and called to someone.

"Are we in trouble?" Erna said, her voice quavering.

"Shshshsh!" Alfreda warned. Before she and her sister could finish dressing, a group of angry stewards gathered outside the changing room door. Erna felt more terrified than ever. *What have I done wrong?* She had not stolen the ring. She had only found it in the tub. *Why are they treating us like criminals?* Over and over she could hear the words being repeated among the stewards: "Sinn Fein."

"Who is this 'Sinn Fein?'" Alfreda whispered to her sister.

Erna trembled. "I don't know."

The girls were pushed along the corridor by the bath attendant. She paused and glanced at them angrily before she rapped on a door. She gave the girls a shove into the room where a man sat behind a desk. He looked up wearily from a pile of papers. His gold-rimmed glasses slipped down his nose.

The bath attendant barked rapid words at the man behind the desk. He nodded and looked at the girls. He examined the ring. He frowned. When he stood up, Alfreda noticed that he was not nearly as tall or as heavy as the bath attendant. But she seemed to treat him with some measure of respect. She did not grab his arm or shout into his face the way she did to the girls.

"Svensk?" he demanded of Erna and Alfreda.

Alfreda nodded, trembling. She felt certain that they were in such terrible trouble that they would be sent back to Sweden as soon as they arrived in America. They were doomed. And she could not tell what they had done. *It's unfair.* More than ever, she wished she could speak English.

The man behind the desk motioned to some chairs. The girls sat down. They waited and waited. The man went about his business with his papers, seemingly forgetting that they were even there. Finally there was a polite knock at the door. A tall, slope-shouldered man wearing a crisp, white steward's coat entered. He slipped his hat from his head and twisted it nervously in his hands. His pale hair stood straight up like summer grass. Reluctantly he turned to Alfreda and her sister. "I am a first-class steward," he said in Swedish. Then he sniffed and frowned. "I don't normally come down to this area of the ship. Please don't waste my time or my superior's. The head steward wants to know where did you find the ring?"

"My sister found the ring in the tub," said Alfreda, eager to speak to someone who could understand her. "You are from Värmland. I can tell by your accent."

The steward blushed. "My superior wishes to know who the ring belongs to."

"I don't know. Neither does my sister," Alfreda said, leaning forward. "When were you last home?"

The steward coughed nervously. "That is none of your business."

"Why does this ring make everyone so frightened?" Alfreda asked.

The Swedish steward glanced at his boss. "The

words on the inside must mean something terrifying to the English."

" 'Sinn Fein?' " Alfreda asked.

As soon as she said this word, the head steward began talking angrily again. He poked his finger at the Swedish steward. "He tells me to ask you what you know about Sinn Fein," the steward said. "I suggest you tell him so you'll avoid terrible trouble." His weary voice sounded kinder now.

"I have never heard the words before," Alfreda said. "Is it someone's name? Perhaps the owner of the ring?"

The steward paused to listen respectfully as his boss rattled off more angry English words. The steward turned to Alfreda. "These words are serious. They represent something that frightens the British. My boss is afraid there is an Irish insurgent on board. A dangerous revolutionary. Someone who will have to go back to England and possibly face a jail sentence."

"Do my sister and I look like dangerous revolutionaries?" Alfreda demanded.

"No," the steward said and blushed again. "But you must understand that Sinn Fein is the name of a group that is suspected of terrorist crimes against the British government. Explosions. Killings." He mopped his forehead with his handker-chief. "Again I must ask you, do you know who this ring belongs to?"

Alfreda shook her head. She nudged her sister. Erna, who had been ignored up until this moment, shook her head, too.

"Perhaps another girlfriend aboard ship? Another passenger you've seen in steerage?" the steward asked wearily.

"We have never seen this ring before," Alfreda said.

Erna nodded. She twisted the hem of her dress. Deep down, she knew who the ring belonged to. But she couldn't say. She felt too afraid. Whenever she looked at her sister, she could see that Alfreda was terribly frightened. She thought about what Mama had said to her before she left. *Obey your sister. Do as she says.*

"Again, one last time, I must ask you," the steward demanded, turning to Erna. "Little sister, do you know who this ring belongs to?"

In perfect Swedish Alfreda hissed Boppa's warning: "Put your feet up on the bench or else the troll will come and bite you."

Erna was so taken aback that her sister remembered the old, familiar phrase, her mouth snapped shut. She exactly knew what her sister was trying to say. *Be quiet. Say nothing.*

"What's that supposed to mean?" the Swedish steward demanded, looking perplexed.

"Don't pay any attention to our old-fashioned country ways," Alfreda said. She batted her eyelashes. "We learn very slowly."

Finally frustrated by the girls' apparent ignorance, the head steward sent away his Swedish translator. Then he dismissed the girls as well. Erna and Alfreda made a little bow. The head steward picked up the ring, looked at it again, then placed it inside a white envelope on his desk.

In silence the two girls hurried down the corridor. They could feel the eyes of many other people in steerage looking at them as they passed. The other passengers whispered as they passed. Alfreda held tight to Erna's hand and marched along as if she didn't notice.

They rounded the corner and scurried past the room where they had taken a bath in the green water. In horror Erna watched as her sister quickly tore something from the wall near the door. She was too frightened to say anything until they reached their room and shut the door. "What did you do?" she whispered. "You destroyed ship property and now we will be in even more trouble."

Alfreda's eyes narrowed. "Our names are on this list." She glanced quickly at the sheet, which showed everyone who had used the bath. "Now I know how important words can be."

Erna did not understand. Horrified, she watched as her sister wadded up the paper, stuffed it inside her pocket and opened the door as if she were leaving. "Where are you going?" Erna said, panicking.

"To the privy. Don't worry. I'll be right back," Alfreda said and vanished.

That was when Erna understood. Her sister was going to flush the paper down, down into the ocean. Wearily Erna lay on her bed. She tried to close her eyes, but she could not sleep. She kept thinking of Mama's warning about being cast overboard and eaten by fish with sharp teeth. *I wish we were safe at home again.*

After what seemed like a very long time, Alfreda returned. She shut the door quietly behind her. To make sure that no one would enter, she leaned against the door and spoke to Erna in a quiet voice. "You know who the ring belongs to, don't you?"

Erna sat up. Guiltily she nodded. "You aren't going to tell, I hope."

Alfreda bit her lip and felt confused. "I never liked her."

Erna slid forward on the bed so that her legs hung over the edge. "She and Bridget aren't so bad. They gave us all their candy."

"So?"

"Remember what Mama said? They punish people at sea by pushing them—"

Alfreda rolled her eyes. "Mama was only trying to frighten you with that fish story."

Erna frowned. She tapped her forehead with the tips of her fingers. She looked down at Boppa's carving on her pillow. Deep down, she knew there was something horrible in what her sister was suggesting. Worse than not feeding the *tomte* or making fun of the *sjörå*. Erna knew that telling on Nora was an act that Alfreda would regret the rest of her life. *I must think of some way to stop her.* "Nora's not so different from you and me," Erna said finally.

"What are you saying? We're nothing like Nora. Or Bridget for that matter."

Erna took a deep breath. She turned the *tomte* over and over again in her hands. "Did you ever think, what happened to Nora could happen to us."

"What do you mean?"

"A mistake. Like Mama's rash. Some authority thinking her spots were something serious when they weren't. And then everything changes. Mama has to stay behind. Well, what if that steward's wrong about the ring? What if Nora's innocent? The words inside the ring will send her back to England. Maybe to jail. That doesn't seem fair, does it?"

Alfreda was silent for several moments. She had never noticed before how wise her sister could be. *Maybe Erna's right. Someday I might need someone to believe in me.* "No use in tempting ill fate." Alfreda smiled, remembering Mama's favorite phrase. *Maybe I'm not as modern and American as I thought.*

Chapter 10

Time seemed to crawl that afternoon as Alfreda and Erna waited for Nora and Bridget's return. Every footstep down the corridor made them jump. Erna tried to nap, but she could not. Alfreda busied herself studying *The Emigrant's Interpreter*. Finally there was a knock at the door.

Erna took a deep breath, terrified that it might be the head steward coming back for them. *Perhaps he found out what Alfreda did with the paper from the wall.*

Bridget and Nora tiptoed into the room. Their hair was still damp. They appeared pale and worried as they glanced quickly up at Erna and Alfreda on their bunk beds. Alfreda cleared her throat and motioned to them. She could see that they were frightened. Softly they closed the door behind themselves.

"I don't think they know what you want," Erna told her sister.

Nora and Bridget perched on the edge of the lower bunk. For once they were not joking or laughing or talking. They studied Alfreda's face carefully. Alfreda pointed to Nora's bare hand, then held up her own hand and pointed to the place where Nora had once worn her ring.

Nora bit her lip. She slid her hand under a fold in her dress as if to hide it. Bridget whispered something to Nora.

Desperately, Alfreda tried to find a phrase in *The Emigrant's Interpreter* to explain in English what she was trying to say. In the section called "At the Station" she read aloud:

"Passengers for the West change cars."

Bridget and Nora looked at each other in confusion.

Alfreda tried again. She read:

"What shall we do?

Get out all of you."

That did not seem right, either. Bridget and Nora glanced nervously at the door. Nora began to cry.

"I can't find the right way to tell them," Alfreda said in frustration.

"Let me try," Erna said. She climbed down off her top bunk and stood in the small, cramped space in the middle of the room. She pretended to be taking a bath. She splashed invisible water on herself and washed her arms and hair and head.

Nora stopped crying and watched carefully.

Erna leaned forward. From the floor she picked up an imaginary object between two fingers. Carefully she examined the object, pretending to slip it on her ring finger.

Nora and Bridget leaned forward in rapt attention.

Now Erna acted out the part of the angry bath attendant. She shook her finger. She scowled. She marched in place holding the invisible ring between her fingers. She pretended to hold the ring up and said, "Sinn Fein."

At the sound of these words, Nora began to cry again. Bridget put her arm around her to comfort her.

Quickly, Alfreda scanned the handbook under the section "On the Ship." She pointed triumphantly and read aloud in English:

"Pooh, there is no danger.

Now the storm is over. Now we shals let you out."

Nora wiped her face with the sleeve of her dress. She looked at Alfreda with a glimmer of hope.

"We have to show we don't intend to tell on her," Erna hissed to her sister.

Bridget and Nora glanced at Erna. Erna pointed to Alfreda. Then she pointed to herself, closed her lips tight, and drew one finger across her mouth. She did the same to her sister.

Bridget gave a half-smile. So did Nora.

Relieved, Alfreda closed her phrase book. Trying to make herself understood was hard work. "Do you think they know what we mean?" Alfreda asked Erna.

Erna shrugged and retreated back to her bunk bed.

Trembling, Nora stood up. She pointed to her hand where the ring had once been. She motioned to her heart. Then she pretended to march like a soldier, very straight, very tall. She even gave a little salute.

"What's she trying to show?" Erna asked her sister.

"I'm not sure," Alfreda replied. "I think she means to tell us that the ring was given to her by someone she loves. A soldier maybe."

"A 'Sinn Fein' soldier," Erna murmured.

When Nora heard this word, she grabbed Erna by the elbow. She touched her heart again. She nodded.

"Her sweetheart gave her the ring," Alfreda said. "I wonder if he's aboard this ship. Maybe he's going to America, too."

"America!" Nora and Bridget said together, smiling.

Erna and Alfreda smiled, too. At last they had discovered a word that all four of them could understand.

That evening at dinner a bustling steward made an announcement in English. Everyone stopped eating. Since Erna and Alfreda were sitting with Berta and Elin, they demanded to know what he was saying.

"He says that anyone who may have lost a gold ring should see him," Berta said importantly.

Alfreda gave Erna a swift warning kick under the table.

"A gold ring?" Elin replied. She took another large bite of yellow cake with frosting. "Who among us would have anything so fine? Was it stolen?"

Berta shrugged. "I can't imagine why anyone

would be stupid enough to lose anything so valuable."

Alfreda coughed. She took a sip of water. Over the top of her glass, she winked at her sister.

The next morning Alfreda woke up early. She heard the two Irish girls whispering worriedly together in their bunks.

"Is it already time to get up?" Erna said in a sleepy voice.

"Rise and shine!" Alfreda called. Then she turned to Nora, who had circles under her eyes. She seemed pale and her hair stood in unkempt tufts on her head. *"Nora, under your pillow look,"* Alfreda instructed.

Nora glanced at her in amazement, as if she were very surprised to hear her speaking in English. Nora slipped her hand under her pillow. Excitedly she produced a small, gold object. She jumped out of bed and pulled on Bridget's blanket to show her. The ring!

Bridget sighed and called down to Alfreda something that sounded like a question.

"I think she's probably wondering how the ring got there," Alfreda said in a low, amused voice. "You'd better tell her."

"Tomte," Erna answered.

"*Tomte?*" Nora replied as if completely perplexed.

Alfreda nodded. "That's right. The *tomte* crept into the head steward's office, found it, and brought it here."

Neither Bridget nor Nora seemed interested in finding out an exact translation with sign language. They were too busy searching their valise and bags for something. Happily Nora sat on the top bunk with her legs crossed and with needle and thread sewed the gold ring safely inside the hem of her dress where no one would ever notice it.

"How did you get the ring back?" Erna demanded, impressed by her sister's cleverness and bravery.

"Remember the Swedish-speaking steward?"

"The homesick one from Värmland?"

Alfreda nodded. "I talked to him after dinner last night. He told me that word had spread quickly in steerage among the Irish about what was engraved inside the ring. No one had dared claim it. The ring was just sitting there on the head steward's desk. When I explained how we had lost almost everything when our dear mother was left behind at Southampton, he felt sorry for us and gave me the ring. 'Finders keepers,' he said."

Erna grinned. "Do you believe that the *tomte* might have had something to do with convincing him?"

"Perhaps," Alfreda said and laughed.

That evening in their room, Erna could not sleep. She sat on her bunk writing a letter. The room was so cold, she had on her clothes with blankets piled on top of her. Every so often she had to rub her hands together to warm them so that she could continue writing:

❧

April 14, 1912

Dear Anna:

You should be surprised to see me now that I am on my way to America. I do not feel so very afraid. The ocean is very vast and for days we have seen no land. The sun shines and even though it is colder today we can still walk along the deck. Did you know my sister Alfreda is very clever folding handkerchiefs into shapes of animals? She and I went exploring and discovered

the booming loud place where the engines
roar. I showed her the ship's six little black-
and-white kittens and she picked out her favorite—a bossy fat one with a white patch
over one eye. We named the whiny scrawny
kitten Klinta-Kitta and the mischievous one
Anna! I hope you will not be angry. So far
this day has been the most wonderful yet.
We have yellow cake for dessert and lovely
ham. I shall be very plump when you see
me next. I wonder if everyone eats so well
in America. Most marvelous of all is my sister's company. I told her the first thing I
want to do when I get to America is take
off my shoes and walk on the sidewalk
made of gold. She says the first thing she
wants to do when we arrive is to eat American ice cream which she has read about in
a newspaper. It is cold and sweet as snow.
This has been a perfect day—the first time
Alfreda treats me like a friend, not just an
annoying pest. So you see perhaps—

❧

Erna stopped writing. She cupped her hands
and blew on them. She sniffed. Her nose was
cold, too. The air had a strange odor. Or was she

just imagining? The smell reminded her of the time she and Anna found a hidden cave. From the entrance came the same clammy, damp smell. Berta had told her they were passing something called icebergs. *What does an iceberg look like? Perhaps tomorrow at daylight I will see one.*

She picked up her pencil to begin to write again when suddenly she paused and listened. A queer shiver rattled through the berth. The door jiggled as if someone on the other side were trying to get in. Startled, Erna called to her sister on the bunk, "What was that?"

Alfreda listened. She had sensed the same odd vibration—almost as if heavy chains were being knocked against the ship. But as quickly as the sensation appeared, it had vanished. "I don't hear anything now. Go back to sleep. It's nothing."

Erna swung over the bunk and stared upside down at her sister. "Something's different. Can't you feel it?"

Alfreda was silent for several moments. *She's so oversensitive.* The low, dull rumbling that they'd felt almost constantly since they'd boarded seemed to have stopped. There was dead silence. Out in the hallway came the crash of doors slamming shut. "Go to sleep," Alfreda said. "I'm sure everything's fine."

Erna folded her letter to Anna and tucked it under her pillow with the *tomte*. She leaned back in bed and shut her eyes. There was a sharp knock at the door. Bridget flew into the room. Her voice was bright and high-pitched. Playfully she tossed a chunk of ice onto Alfreda's bed. *"Iceberg!"* she said gaily. *"Iceberg!"*

Alfreda laughed and tossed the ice to the floor. Erna was about to leap from her bunk to inspect Bridget's gift, when she noticed the silent, thin stream of water flowing under the doorway. It was coming from the corridor.

Suddenly Berta arrived, breathless. She was wearing a strange thick, white vest over her clothing. "Have you seen Elin?" she asked Alfreda. "I cannot find her anywhere. They say the ship has struck an iceberg."

Alfreda swung her legs down off the bed. The room was very crowded. Bridget and Berta had to go out into the watery hallway so that Erna and Alfreda could climb down off their beds. An impatient steward stood in the corridor. He shoved three life belts into the room for Alfreda, her sister, and Bridget. He barked something in English.

"What did he say?" Alfreda asked Berta.

" 'Follow the rest upstairs,' " Berta replied. "I

don't know what the fuss is about. The ship is unsinkable. But we might as well do as he says."

"Come along, Erna," Alfreda said. "This sounds like an adventure."

From out in the corridor came a babble of voices as the other people from steerage seemed to be gathering their bags and worldly belongings. Babies cried. Sleepy children called out to their parents. Alfreda put the life belt over her sister's head and cinched it tight.

"It's uncomfortable," Erna complained.

"Never mind. Come on. Let's go up on deck. Perhaps Elin is already there," Alfreda said.

"Should we take our belongings?" Erna asked, thinking of the *tomte* under her pillow.

"I'm sure we'll be back in just a little while. Nothing to worry about. You coming, Bridget?" Alfreda said, motioning to the Irish girl. Bridget did not seem to be the least bit frightened.

Erna, Alfreda, Bridget, and Berta sloshed through the water in the corridor toward the stairs. Alfreda held her sister's hand tightly as a family of Italians lumbered past carrying a huge bundle. Some chatted. Some joked and laughed. No one seemed worried. Alfreda had second thoughts about going back for their belongings. *What if someone wanders in and robs us while we're above deck?* She paused to turn around, but a crowd blocked her way back down the stairs again.

"What are you doing?" Erna demanded.

"Nothing. Come on. Keep walking," Alfreda said.

The black night sky was filled with stars. There was no wind. The sea all around them seemed as calm as a pond back home. Erna looked all around. "Where's the iceberg?" she asked her sister.

"I don't see anything," Alfreda replied, peering into the distance. "I'm cold and tired. I want to go back to bed where it's warm."

Shouts echoed across the far end of the deck. A group of boys gaily kicked pieces of ice back and forth to each other as if enjoying a game. Breathlessly Bridget and Nora ran up to Erna, Alfreda, and Berta to show them an enormous chunk of ice. The girls smiled and laughed. A taller young man with a cap stood behind Nora. He grabbed her hand and pulled her toward the ice-kicking game. Alfreda suspected that he must be the boyfriend who had given Nora the troublesome gold ring. Bridget lost interest in standing on the deck with the three Swedish girls and hurried to join Nora and her boyfriend.

"Look at that!" Alfreda cried. Far below them they heard splashing. A tiny boat rowed past, barely half full. The bright lights from the *Titanic* revealed clearly that these were passengers. They were all wearing the same pale, ghostly life belts.

"It's just a precaution, I'm sure," Berta said. "They'll send everyone out in the lifeboats to catch a chill, then call them all back again."

"But what about the water downstairs in our room?" Erna asked nervously. The ocean looked very big, black, and cold. She did not want to go out in one of those tiny boats with oars. Neither she nor Alfreda could swim. *Isn't it safer staying on the big ship?*

"Oh, the crew's probably already mopping up the water down below," Berta said and laughed. "A little puddle—that's nothing. It's no worse than the floods back home after the river rises in the spring, is it?"

Alfreda chuckled. "On Alna we get used to going about with wet feet."

Erna watched fascinated as the fancy ladies from first class shrieked and laughed in their life belts. *They look just like us now.* Some of the children from first class looked as if they were wearing flimsy nightgowns. Some of their mothers wore shiny, silk evening dresses. A boy from steerage tried to show off by clambering up the ladders on the sides of the deck up to first class. *What's he doing?* Before he could hand a chunk of ice to one of the top-hatted gentlemen who was smoking a cigar, a steward in a white coat leaned over and shooed him away. The steward pointed down into the steerage area.

"What a rude boy!" Berta said and made a clucking noise with her tongue. "Doesn't he know he should stay in his own area?"

"I think we should go back down to our room and try to gather up some of our things," Erna said. "I'm freezing. We can find some warmer clothes maybe—"

"Maybe Elin's down there," Alfreda interrupted.

The two sisters and Berta headed back down the stairs again toward their room. They were stopped by a steward coming up the steps in a hurry. His face was red and he said something in a warning tone of voice to the girls as he passed.

"He says 'You know she's sinking. Get out while there's time.' He must be trying to scare us," Berta said. "This ship can't sink."

Chapter 11

Everything seemed calm and quiet belowdecks. There was no sound. The *Titanic* appeared as still as if it were tied at the dock back in Southampton. But when the girls scrambled down the last flight of stairs, they saw that the water had crept up to the third step. For several moments they watched the rippling cold gray seawater and did not know what to do.

Another crew member with a blackened face and a dirty shirt sloshed down the corridor toward them. He was waving his arms for them to go back up the steps again. He did not pause as he hurried past them, smelling of coal dust and sweat and kerosene fumes.

"I think . . . I think we'd better go back up on the deck for a little while longer," Alfreda said. "We can come back later—"

"Elin," Berta said, her voice trembling slightly. "Where's Elin? Come on. We've got to find her."

Reluctantly Erna followed her sister and Berta up to the deck again. She would rather have waded through the water to their room. She wanted to go back and make sure their belongings were all right. But she couldn't. She had to do what Alfreda said. *What about the* tomte? She prayed Boppa's carving would be all right until she returned.

When they made their way back to the deck, Berta found a third-class steward and asked him an urgent question. He pointed to the topmost deck in the far distance where the lifeboats were being loaded. "He says that passengers are being loaded from up there," Berta explained. "First-class passengers only."

Alfreda peered into the distance. "What about us?"

"He didn't say," Berta said quietly.

Alfreda frowned. She figured that to make their way up to that distant level would mean getting around the water-tight bulkheads that separated steerage from second and first class. There was no direct, easy route from steerage to the decks with the lifeboats. They'd first have to descend into the ship again, find the right connecting corridors, and make their way forward to the other end of the ship through first and second class — past many gates and signs forbidding their entry.

"What should we do?" Erna said.

"Maybe we should wait here, and when the time is right they'll lower lifeboats for steerage," Berta said. "There's nothing to do but wait."

Alfreda and her sister decided to follow Berta's advice. The girls wandered into the Third-Class Smoking Room, where it was warm. Someone played the piano. A baby cried. A large group of Italian men, women, and children perched on their bundles. Some of the older women in kerchiefs sobbed and cried out a word that Erna could not understand. It sounded like, *"Maria! Maria! Maria!"*

Some of the single men played cards. Others joked and laughed and drank. A bored group, who obviously had been drinking, thought the sight of the wailing, praying Italians was very funny. They joined hands and began to dance in a great circle around them. Others pointed and gestured. They waved their hands in the air as if arguing what to do next.

"I don't want to stay in here," Erna said, tugging on her sister's arm. "It's too noisy."

Alfreda sighed. What harm was there in trying to find their way through the ship to the lifeboats? "Let's go, Berta," she announced.

"Where?" demanded Berta, who had found a comfortable chair near a handsome young man with a blond mustache.

"To the lifeboats," Alfreda explained.

"You go ahead. I'm staying here," Berta said.

Alfreda took her sister's hand. Obediently Erna followed. The route made no sense to her. Why were they going down when they needed to go *across?* What could Alfreda be thinking? But she could not complain or ask her sister anything. She was afraid even to pause and ask her sister the question that had been bothering her for the past half hour. *Is the floor crooked?*

The girls scrambled down the steps and followed a corridor, past more people from steerage who had decided to stay in their rooms. There seemed to be no commotion, no panic. A woman looked up at them as they passed her cabin. She was reading a book.

"Come on!" Alfreda urged Erna. They climbed up another flight of steps and came to a closed gate with a sign that they could not read. Alfreda rattled the gate. A steward appeared on the other side. He was wearing a white coat. He shook his head and said something in English that neither Alfreda nor Erna could understand. "Open the gate!" Alfreda demanded.

The steward would not budge.

"Maybe it's second class," Erna said as helpfully as she could. "Maybe we should go back."

"No," Alfreda replied angrily. "We'll find another way. Another gate that's open."

They had to walk down another flight of stairs and along another corridor. Alfreda had no idea where they were going, only that they were moving forward in the ship in the direction of the stern. By now she was certain. *The ship is tilting.* She did not want to mention this to Erna for fear of alarming her. "Hurry up!" Alfreda said.

They climbed up another set of stairs and again faced a locked gate. Alfreda rattled the gate as hard as she could.

"You better not destroy ship property," Erna said. "We'll be in trouble again."

"Be quiet and help me," Alfreda replied. The girls tugged and tugged, but they could not open the five-foot-tall gate. A man with a white coat hurried past on the other side. Alfreda called to him. "Come back!"

He vanished.

Erna slumped against the wall. "Now what?"

Alfreda shouted louder for help. Another steward appeared.

Erna sighed. *Why would this one be any different?*

However, this time her sister was speaking in rapid Swedish. "Open up! Please? Yes, you remember us?" Alfreda pleaded. "We must get to the lifeboats."

When Erna looked at his face, she recognized him. He was the first-class steward who was homesick. He smiled shyly at Alfreda and quickly unlocked the gate. She and Erna rushed through. They were followed by a group of swarthy, dark-haired men from steerage, who had gathered nearby the gate when they'd heard Alfreda shouting.

Alfreda thanked the steward and raced past, tugging Erna along behind. A steward Erna did not recognize waved them on to follow him. He shepherded them up through a place so amazing that Erna could hardly believe her eyes. Doors had been flung open, revealing the contents just as the first-class passengers left them: a silver slipper on the floor where it had been kicked off, a sparkling necklace dumped on a table, a silky green dress rumpled on the chair. How thrilling to see the fancy rooms lit up so brilliantly—and no one there!

Beneath Erna's feet the carpeting was so thick that it seemed as soft as pine needles in the deepest part of the forest back home. She could not hear her steps as she walked. The smell reminded her of Grandmother's garden in high summer— sweet scents of flowers and wild roses.

A grand, sweeping staircase decorated in wood and gold seemed to go up and up forever. Lights like a thousand icicles shimmered overhead. A statue of a small, fat child on the stairway reminded Erna of a bewitched foundling—half-human, half-troll. She felt as if she had entered a fantastic magical castle.

The fancy folk in life belts wandered past her and Alfreda as if they were invisible. *No one cares we're trespassing!* The dazed first-class passengers walked up the staircase as if they were bewitched. They neither noticed nor cared that Erna curtsied respectfully.

Unlike her sister, Alfreda did not waste her time with curtsies. She was too busy inspecting the tall ceilinged room paneled in deep, gleaming wood. Feathery plants in pots decorated the room. She thought the first-class passengers seemed as quiet and orderly as if they were going to church. So engrossed in their surroundings, she soon lost sight of the steward who had been leading them. *Where has he gone?*

Desperately Alfreda grabbed her sister's hand and followed the sound of music. Someone was playing a cheerful tune on violins. The music floated off the deck into the black night. "There they are," she said to Erna as she scanned the deck. *Where are the other lifeboats? How will there be enough for Elin and Nora and Bridget and Berta and—*

Suddenly the floor shifted beneath their feet. Someone screamed. The band kept playing. *How pleasant.* Erna would have liked to have stood and listened when her sister rudely grabbed her arm and pulled her toward a lifeboat. When Alfreda motioned to the crew member that she and her sister wanted to get in, he pointed to the other side of the ship.

The lights had begun to burn lower and redder. Boat after boat was lowered on ropes and pulleys that hung from wooden outstretched poles. Occasionally the lifeboat ropes jammed. The boat tipped. The passengers screamed. Quick work by the sailors and other men righted the boat. As soon as the boat had landed in the water, it was quickly rowed out of sight.

"I won't get on the boat," a fat Swedish woman on deck cried. "I've never been in a boat like this before."

Someone shoved her in. A man's voice shouted orders, and the men in the lowering boat struggled with the oars. A baby shrieked. Someone passed the screaming bundle down to waiting arms. The men in the boat continued to argue. One man rolled up his sleeves as if he meant to punch the other one.

Erna watched the people—some calm, some hysterical. Some refused to get into the lifeboats. Couples were parted. Gentlemen made brave attempts to say farewell, but as soon as the lifeboats were lowered and the men turned away, she saw their frightened expressions. Some men crawled into the lifeboats. Others leaped in at the last minute as if determined to save themselves.

Erna had her eyes wide open and noticed everything that was going on, but she could not feel any sorrow—or even fear. She felt as if she were part of an audience in a wonderful, dramatic spectacle. Nothing seemed real.

"Erna! Alfreda!"

Erna and her sister turned in time to see Berta approach. Behind her was the young man from the Third-Class Smoking Lounge. He smiled grandly. "This fellow showed me a shortcut up here," Berta said. Her hand fluttered to her hair, which was falling to one side a bit. "His name is August Wennerstrom. He is from a village near my family's."

August bowed from the waist. Suddenly rockets roared white streamers of sparks across the night sky. The girls looked up, astonished. "What's that?" Alfreda asked, wondering if this was yet one more entertainment for the upperclass folk. The noise was deafening. Erna felt the ship tip farther to one side, knocking her off balance. Had the explosion caused the ship to move?

August flicked his cigar ash. "Distress call," he said in Swedish.

"Distress?" Berta said, her face suddenly drawn.

"If there are any ships in the area that see these rocket flares," August said with some authority, "they will come to our aid immediately."

Something about the sound of the rockets and the sight of the pale upturned faces of passengers made Erna's hands sweat. "What about my *tomte?*" Erna moaned. "What about Jenny's baby?"

"Who's Jenny?" Berta asked.

"A cat with kittens in the kitchen," Alfreda said. She spotted another boat being loaded. A man shouted angrily at an older boy who dodged and jumped in with the women. Someone tossed the boy out. Another rocket soared and illuminated the terrified faces on deck. That was when Alfreda remembered. *The railway tickets and all the money.* She had left everything behind in their cabin!

The three girls left August, who seemed busy arguing with two other passengers about how many more boats were already on their way to save them. A man loading passengers on the lifeboats shouted something. His face was covered with sweat even though the night was very cold and he was only wearing a cotton shirt and no life belt.

"What's he saying?" Alfreda asked.

" 'Any more women and children?' " Berta replied.

There was a loud *squeak squeak squeak* as the lifeboat began being lowered to the water. A man carrying a squalling baby rushed toward the railing. He called down. Someone in the lifeboat signaled to him. He tossed the baby into the boat. A woman caught it. The baby shrieked louder.

Suddenly four men with dark hair rushed to the railing and tried to crowd into the packed boat. Someone stood up. A shot rang out. A woman screamed. Another group of men pounced on the men from steerage who had tried to sneak on the boat. They pulled them off by their legs. The men from steerage scampered away and vanished.

"Get on, Erna. Get on this lifeboat!" Alfreda shouted. She knew they had to hurry. This might be their last chance. She shoved her reluctant sister toward the lifeboat.

Erna glanced downward. It was a long, long way to the cold, black water. The lifeboat seemed so small, so fragile. How easily might it be smashed to pieces? Wasn't it safer to stay in the *Titanic?* Nothing would happen. It couldn't sink. "I can't get in," she told Alfreda.

"Yes, you can," Berta hissed in her ear. "Come on. We'll get in together." Berta called out something in perfect English to the man. As soon as he heard her, he waved to the men lowering the boat. They stopped. The man moved swiftly toward the girls. Berta linked arms with Erna. Alfreda pushed Erna from behind. The man grabbed Erna as if she were as light as a bag of goose feathers and hoisted her into the boat. Then he picked up Berta and tossed her in, too.

Alfreda took a step forward, but the man held

his hand up. He motioned to her that there was no more room.

"Alfreda!" Erna shouted. Her face turned upward. She tried to stand. She reached out for the side of the boat, but someone cursed her and pulled her hard and made her sit down.

"I'll come on the next boat!" Alfreda called to her. "I promise!"

The lifeboat jerked and chittered down the cables little by little. Because the big ship tilted, the lifeboat snagged and bumped into the rivets along the side of the ship. The lifeboat's five crew members barked orders at one another. They reached out and pushed away the slow-moving lifeboat from the ship's hull. Inch by inch the lifeboat crept toward the surface of the water. Finally it hit with a soft splash. There was much fumbling with the oars as the tightly packed boat was rowed away.

Erna could barely move. She sat shoulder to shoulder with Berta on one side and a sobbing woman on the other. With great effort she turned to look up. *The next lifeboat. Where was the next lifeboat?* She kept her eyes on the *Titanic,* as bright as a glowworm. Even the windows already underwater still glowed and made the water green and mysterious and evil. The faint notes of the band continued like the eerie sound of *sjörå*.

To keep her mind off her worst fears, she counted the decks by the rows of lights. *One-two-three-four-five-six*. The ship made a low, mourning wail. She counted again. *One-two-three-four-five*. What had happened? Maybe she'd missed one deck. *One-two-three-four*. Only four decks now. *Four*. The *Titanic* was sinking. The great, unsinkable ship was actually going down.

Alfreda! She had to have escaped. Erna knew somehow she'd make it. Alfreda was tough. She was clever. She'd survive, wouldn't she?

No one spoke in the lifeboat. Some people kept their eyes closed and looked as if they were praying. Others covered their faces with their hands. Erna tried not to think of those people she had just left—alive and breathing just like she was. *Elin. Bridget. Nora. Nora's boyfriend. The man from Ireland. And what about Jenny and the kittens?* Erna blinked hard. She counted. *One-two-three*. At that moment the *Titanic* rumbled, groaned and began to upend—still ablaze with light. Wrenching explosions boomed across the water. Sparks shot skyward. The lifeboat oarsmen rowed faster, more desperate than ever to escape.

Even as they moved away from the great, dying

ship, Erna could hear cries from the *Titanic*. Hundreds and hundreds of human voices—a chorus of fear and hopelessness and suffering that reminded her of winter wind scouring the tops of pine trees or the sound of locusts on a midsummer night. Suddenly a dark shape surged across the ship. Erna stared, horrified, as a mass of humanity from steerage surged up onto the deck.

Too late.

All the lifeboats were gone.

Alfreda, almost as if in a dream, watched from the *Titanic* as her sister vanished. There were no more lifeboats. She knew it. The *Titanic* shifted again. *How will I save myself?* She turned, ready to make a dash to the other side of the ship, but found her way blocked by an even larger surge of steerage passengers who had crawled up the companionway and the deck ladders from deep below. She spied an entire third-class family—a father, mother, and six terrified children—who had waited obediently in the Third-Class Smoking Room. Water engulfed the deck. In the blink of an eye the family vanished.

Alfreda scrambled, fell, but somehow managed to escape the enormous wave's grip. She clambered up a railing and hugged tight to the metal even as the ship began to tip crazily. Lights flickered.

The *Titanic*'s stern lifted up, up, up until the ship pointed straight toward the stars like some giant's black accusing finger. The lights snapped off. In one smooth, slow motion the ship slipped downward into the water. Metal grated, gurgled. China crashed. Glass exploded. Steam hissed.

Vibrations convulsed through Alfreda's arms as every movable object inside the ship—from china teacup to grand piano—broke loose, hurled, and slammed down through the hull. Everywhere she glanced she saw people clinging together in clusters and bunches like swarming bees. *If only we had wings.*

Wooden deck chairs and barrels flew past her. Then bodies with legs and arms waving. *Splash! Splash!* She had only seconds. She knew it. With all her strength, she pushed herself away from the ship, held her nose, and leaped into the deadly cold water.

Chapter 12

"It's gone," Berta whispered.

The oarsmen paused. Erna and the others in the crowded lifeboat turned and listened as an awful moan rose up from the wreckage. Somewhere in the darkness a thousand souls cried, prayed, yelled. The oarsmen pulled hard and hurried away, unwilling to return to pick up any survivors.

Some of the women in the lifeboat called back in frantic, pleading voices. Erna could not understand their words. Overwhelmed by their cries of distress, some passengers held their hands over their ears.

"Shouldn't we go back?" Erna protested. In the reflection of the stars she saw gently rocking pieces of debris—floating boxes and doors and chairs and tables. A top hat. A doll. And bodies. More bodies than she could count. *Alfreda. Where is Alfreda?*

"We have no room," Berta hissed. "If we go back, all those people will swamp the boat. Then we'll drown, too. Shut up and sit still."

"*Tsssssk!*" clucked the shivering old Swedish woman who sat hunched in front of Erna. "Do not plague us with your quarrels. You should thank God you are the lucky ones. Sisters who still have each other."

Erna sighed. *Sisters?* She wanted to tell the woman that Berta was not her sister. *Her* sister was on another lifeboat. But she had neither the energy nor the courage to explain. Instead, she peered silently at the distant, smoky place where the *Titanic* had upended and disappeared. She could see her breath. Her hands and feet felt numb. Back home in winter the water beneath the crust of frozen fjords and lakes pierced the lungs like fire. *No one can survive out there for long.*

The cries seemed fainter, weaker now. Soon they disappeared altogether. The silence was horrible.

The baby, who had been whimpering, was handed to the woman next to Erna. The fretting worsened. Erna took the wiggling bundle, which smelled sour and felt damp. She could not see the motherless child's face, but she could tell that its blanket was too flimsy for the cold. She wrapped the baby as best she could, making sure its feet were covered with part of her skirt. She held it close and rocked it back and forth the way she used to lull Karl to sleep. Little by little, the baby stopped squirming. Erna listened to its regular, rapid breathing and felt grateful to have something to keep her mind occupied.

In the distance shone a light—perhaps another ship. Slowly the lifeboat moved toward it. But somehow the light never seemed to grow any closer. Which direction were they headed?

There was no compass on the boat. They had no food, water, or lantern. The wind turned icy. Waves rocked the lifeboat. Erna's stomach lurched. She rubbed her hands together and stamped her feet gently, trying not to think about throwing up. She held the baby close. Still she did not feel any warmer. *What if the baby's freezing, too?*

Few people in the lifeboat spoke. Some sat and stared into space. Some prayed. Some sobbed. Erna's head nodded. She tried to sleep, but she couldn't. She wished she had her *tomte*—something familiar and comforting. Something that might make her think of home. A cry rang out. There was a thud. Erna could not see anything

167 ◆

in the darkness. She heard angry voices. *Thump!*
Thump! The boat rocked. A woman screamed.
One of the men who was rowing shouted. It
sounded as if he were cursing someone.

"What's happening?" Erna whispered, tugging
on Berta's sleeve.

Berta wiped her mouth with her hand. "Four
stowaways up front. Chinamen who hid under
the seats. They are being beaten."

"Why?" Erna demanded.

"Only women and children were supposed to
board."

What difference does it make now? "Will they be
thrown out into the water?" Erna asked in confusion.

Berta shrugged as if she did not care.

When there was no splash, Erna felt relieved.
She wished she could see these Chinamen. Did
they have pigtails? She marveled that any grown-
up could make himself so small as to fit under
the seat of a lifeboat. *Perhaps Alfreda thought of some
equally clever way to survive.*

Little by little, streaks of light illuminated the
eastern horizon. For the first time Erna and the
others could see that they were surrounded by jag-
ged masses of glistening white and gray icebergs.
To Erna, these frozen formations looked like sinister
troll castles. In every direction stretched water and

ice. The baby woke and whimpered. Erna let it hungrily suck on her knuckle.

The distant light they had followed all night was gone. They were hopelessly lost. Someone wept softly. Another woman began to mutter. As if sensing that the group was losing hope, the oarsmen began to sing. As they pulled the oars, they chanted:

"Pull for the shore, sailor, pull for the shore!
Heed not the rolling waves, but bend to the oar."

To amuse the baby, Erna sang along with them. She had no idea what they were singing. Somehow she felt convinced that Alfreda would be pleased when she heard her speak these English sailor words.

"Be quiet, will you?" Berta complained. "Must I listen to you *and* that brat howl?"

"Sorry," Erna murmured. She stopped practicing her English.

Hours seemed to drag by. The baby slept fitfully. Cold cut through Erna's thin, cotton clothes. Her back and legs felt stiff and sore. Suddenly someone shouted and pointed a finger at a spot on the horizon. A ship! Everyone turned eagerly to study the black shape that seemed to be growing larger.

Yes, it's coming closer! The oarsmen pulled harder now. Some of the women searched the bottom of the lifeboat for anything to burn—a straw hat, a scarf. One of the women found a wad of letters in her pocket. She lit these with matches and held the burning papers high in the air. The fire quickly burned out. Charred ash floated in a heap in the water. Everyone in the lifeboat began shouting and waving.

Now at last I'll see Alfreda again.

Once the lifeboat skirted the last cluster of icebergs, Erna could read the ship's name: *Carpathia.* *Such a beautiful word!* Sheltered on the side of the ship out of the way of the growing waves, the men finally stopped rowing. Ropes and rope ladders were dropped down from the enormous ship. One by one each passenger struggled to grab the ropes and fit the noose around her shoulders to help climb up. Some of the passengers were too tired or weak even to fasten the rope around themselves. The crying baby was lifted aboard inside a canvas mail pouch.

When it was Erna's turn, she found herself hurtling up into the air. She feared she might fly straight into the ship's side. She screamed. Someone from above called down. The rest of her journey proceeded much more slowly. When she reached the deck of the *Carpathia*, someone grabbed her. She did not feel anything. Her feet were so numb, she could not walk. Speechless, she stood as someone quickly wrapped her in a blanket. She saw someone carrying the baby. She did not have to worry about its safety anymore. The baby would be fed and given some warm, dry clothes. Still, she wondered. *What is its name? Where is its mother?*

Erna limped across the deck to a man with a clipboard. He asked her a question, then paused with his pencil ready to mark the paper. Erna could not understand him. She shook her head. Tears formed in her eyes. The man rattled through a list of words. Finally, he said, *"Svensk?"*

Erna nodded. She knew that word.

"Namne?" he asked.

"Anderson," she said.

He glanced through his list again. "Alfreda Anderson?"

Erna began to cry. She couldn't help herself. She wanted her sister. Where was her sister?

"Alfreda Anderson?" he repeated, clearly impatient.

Erna shook her head. She pointed to herself. "Erna Anderson."

He scribbled something on the paper. Boldly she grabbed his arm. "Alfreda Anderson?" she demanded, desperate to see if her sister had been saved and brought aboard.

The man checked his list and shook his head. He turned to a kind-looking woman and gave another order. The woman took Erna by the arm. She put something around her neck. A string with a little cardboard sign that said, *"SWEDEN?"* Erna followed the woman to a warm place inside the ship where everyone was smiling and offering her steaming bowls of soup and mugs of coffee. No one mentioned the *Titanic*. No one spoke of the disaster.

Why are they smiling? Don't they know what just happened? Angrily Erna slurped hot soup. As her feet and hands began to feel warmer, she felt incredibly tired. She wanted to sleep, but she could not. She had to watch for Alfreda.

Erna hobbled back to the deck railing. She watched another lifeboat unload below. It took a very long time for everyone to be hoisted aboard. Anxiously she watched for every new arrival, certain that this one would be her sister. Each time she was disappointed. Other women lined the railing, too. Each one stared longingly in the distance. Rarely someone came aboard and was greeted with hugs and screams and tears. Most often the women lining the railing waited and waited. Their husbands, their sons, their loved ones never appeared.

After many long hours Erna counted twenty lifeboats. Twenty lifeboats had been unloaded on to the *Carpathia*. The women at the railing stared out to sea even when there were no more lifeboats to be seen.

A woman pleaded in frantic Swedish to a *Carpathia* crew member, "My husband is out there. He said he was coming on the next boat. He promised!"

The crew member could not understand her. He shrugged apologetically and pulled up the rope ladders and coiled them carefully. The *Carpathia*'s engines started up, and the ship began its long, slow search of the *Titanic* wreckage. The ship circled but found no living survivors. Eventually other search ships arrived. *Carpathia* turned and began steaming away.

Erna felt numb. This wasn't really happening. Her sister had been picked up and was safe on another ship. Perhaps a faster-moving ship than the *Carpathia*. She was sure of it. When they docked in New York, she would find Alfreda.

"Has Elin come aboard?" Berta asked.

Erna shook her head sadly. "I haven't seen Bridget or Nora, either. I am looking for Alfreda." Someone's hand pressed on Erna's shoulder. She turned, hopeful.

It wasn't Alfreda.

The figure looked vaguely familiar. It was the complaining old Swedish woman from their lifeboat. She clamped her strong, clawlike hand on Berta's shoulder, too. "You should thank the Lord for your good fortune."

"What good fortune?" Erna asked.

"That the Almighty, bless His name, thought fit to save two sisters," the woman replied. She looked at Erna as if she were either very ungrateful or very stupid. "Get down on your knees and pray."

"She . . . she's not my sister," Erna said, her voice trembling.

"She's not?" the woman replied. She turned to Berta. "You said you were sisters."

Berta looked indignant. "Old mother, you're mistaken—"

"When you got on the lifeboat. I heard you plain as day. I was right there. You spoke English. I understood every word. 'There must be room for us,' you said. 'We're sisters.' I haven't lost my hearing or my mind yet, thank the good Lord. Praise His name."

Berta blushed. "Ignore her, Erna. She's crazy," she whispered. She tugged hard on her arm as if to drag her out of earshot of the woman.

Erna would not budge. She stared incredulously at Berta the liar. Berta the trickster. The one who had taken Alfreda's place on the lifeboat. "How could you?"

Berta let go of Erna's arm. "What do you care? *You* are alive, aren't you?"

Erna felt as if all the air had been knocked out of her. She doubled over and stumbled. *Have to get away. Get away.* In her haste, she tripped headlong into the woman who had given her soup. The woman acted as if Erna were sick. She gently led her to the *Carpathia* saloon, which was packed with makeshift beds for the women passengers. Erna recognized no one. The other people from steerage did not speak. They huddled in a daze, not caring that tags with words hung around each of their necks.

Erna lay down on one of the piles of neatly folded blankets. She pressed her face against the scratchy, mildewed wool. But her eyes would not close. She could not sleep.

Four days later in darkness and rolling seas, the *Carpathia* approached the New York harbor. The wind howled. Rain poured. Impatiently Erna stared out the fogged saloon window. She rubbed the glass with her dirty sleeve but could not see

America—only more grayness, more rain. *Alfreda's waiting for me. She'll know what we should do next.*

Lightning flashed. The sudden, cruel blast of light reminded Erna of the warning flares that had soared overhead before the *Titanic* sank. She shielded her eyes and felt as if she might throw up. No matter how hard she tried, she could not stop her uncontrollable trembling.

A dozen tugboat horns blasted. Men shouted through megaphones from smaller boats that trailed alongside the *Carpathia*. The arrival seemed to take forever. Finally the ship stopped. A great roar came from the dock. When Erna opened the window, she saw thousands and thousands of waiting people. She gulped. How would she find her sister among such a huge crowd? More bright lights flashed from the docks. Men with small black boxes pointed at the gangplank called out and waved their hats as the first-class passengers descended first, followed by second class. Staccato shrieks and pitiful wails filled the air.

Erna waited, shivering, with the other steerage passengers as special inspectors from Ellis Island boarded the ship to check their eyes, their hearts yet again. They asked them questions Erna could not understand. *When will they let me go?* Desperately she craned her neck—trying to catch sight of her sister.

At last she was free to walk down the canopied gangplank. More blinding flashes. A band played somewhere. Voices called to her, *"Survivor? Survivor?"* Someone else coming down the gangplank prodded her back to hurry. She stumbled, terrified. The roar was deafening. She could not hear, she could not think. *Where is Alfreda?* Erna stood on the dock. Her legs felt rubbery and strange. Eight days had passed since she'd left Southampton. Eight endless days. She waited, alone and terrified.

A woman with a sign pinned to her uniform briskly approached her. She spoke to her in English and Erna could not understand what she wanted. Gently she led Erna to a group of women standing behind a table heaped with cast-off clothing. *What does she want me to do?* Erna bit her lip. The woman pointed and made an offering motion with her hand. "Take what you want," the woman said in Swedish. "I am from the Swedish Immigration Society."

The beaming woman handed her a too-big, plaid coat and a hideous gray flannel hat. Even though Erna's flimsy dress was damp and soiled, she did not want any of these America-clothes. The woman offered her a steaming mug of coffee.

Erna did not want any America-coffee. All she wanted was Alfreda.

Still her sister did not come for her.

What should I do? She had no money, no train tickets. She owned nothing except the clothes on her back. The *tomte*—everything—was gone. She did not know where she was supposed to meet her uncle Fred. She did not know what he looked like.

"Alfreda Anderson?" she asked the cheerful Swedish Immigration Society woman. The woman looked through a list she held clipped to a board. The list was typed and all around the edges was an ominous black border. "Anderson, Alfreda," she said at last. She looked down at Erna. Now her eyes were sorrowful. She shook her head.

Erna's heart thudded in her throat. She forgot to breathe. She stood dumbfounded. *Alfreda told Mama she'd always take care of me. She promised.* "Look again," Erna told the woman.

Reluctantly the woman did as she was told. She pointed to the words on the list. Erna could see her sister's name for herself. A-L-F-R-E-D-A. Erna squinted, unable to hear the woman speak or the band play. Even the constant, hungry roar from the crowd faded inside her head. *Alone. Now you are alone.*

Chapter 13

The Swedish Immigration Society building was clean and crowded with other people who had recently come to America. Erna and the other women and children slept in one big room filled with squeaking iron cots. They ate in another room with the men. Sometimes they were served familiar food like potatoes and *lutfisk*, fish boiled in water until it tasted papery. People came. People went. Berta, who lingered a few days after the *Carpathia* unloaded, vanished one day. She did not say goodbye. She simply slipped out into the crowded, noisy streets of New York and never came back.

Erna waited, uncertain what to do. "You are

famous," one of the Immigration Society cooks told her. "You survived the *Titanic.*"

Erna did not want to be famous. She wanted to be home again. She wanted Mama and her grandparents. At night she dreamed of green trees dappled in sunlight, moving in the wind. In New York there were no woods. There were no *tomtar.* No one believed in magic. Alfreda had been right.

Erna kept to herself and seldom spoke to anyone. Sometimes she helped rock crying babies. Sometimes she did laundry. She liked to peel potatoes and hang out blankets high on the roof in the sunlight. These things reminded her of home. But she knew that the New York sunlight wasn't Swedish sunlight. Nothing was really the same.

The weather turned hot and unbearably muggy. The America-summer made Erna sweat the way she never had before. The pulsing, relentless heat filled the building and made sleep impossible. Nights were starless, moonless. The sluggish, foul air outdoors barely moved. What she could see of the sky overhead appeared milky white gray from so much smoke and soot. She longed to hear a bird sing, to hear a brook babble. But all she heard were the clatter of traffic and the constant cry of street vendors.

Little by little she began to forget what home looked like. At night she tried very hard to remember. But the images had begun to fade around the edges. Even Mama's face wavered and vanished. Only Boppa remained vivid. *And of course Alfreda.* She didn't like to think of her sister too much. The thought was too painful.

One day Miss Asplund, the head of the Swedish Immigration Society, called Erna into her office. She had restless, blue-veined hands and a thin, pious expression that reminded Erna of a bald-faced hornet. "Erna Anderson," she said briskly, "why don't you write to your family in Sweden?"

"I tried once, ma'am," Erna said and curtsied. "No one ever answered."

"Try again."

"Yes, ma'am," Erna said halfheartedly. *Boppa can't read.* Erna didn't want to tell Miss Asplund for fear she'd pity her even more. She went back to her cot and sat down with a piece of paper and a pencil. She wrote:

Summer 1912

She did not know the exact date. She peered out the window. Overhead the sun beat down unmercifully between the tall, sooty buildings. Back home it must be nearly the midsummer holiday—the day the sun never seemed to set. She remembered last year how she and Anna went into the meadow and gathered wildflowers to decorate the house. There was a maypole in the village and dancing and fragrant thorny roses in the church. After midsummer came haymaking. She sighed and picked up her pencil again.

❧

Dear Boppa:

Please answer this I beg you. I am trapped in New York where I know not one single soul. Uncle Fred never arrived. My father I cannot remember and he would scarce recognize me. By now you must have heard of what happened to our ship and dearest Alfreda. I think now I understand what you meant by a real sacrifice. I believe she gave up her own life for me. How I miss her! At the Immigration Society people are kind. I peel potatoes and help with laundry and sweep out the dining room. But I am miserable unhappy in this crowded city. There are no trees. The air chokes me with smoke and

I cannot understand what people say. Every day I wait for a familiar face to appear at the door. None comes. Please send for me and let me return to Sweden. I will even cross the ocean again, though I dread it. Do you hear from Mama? Did she come home? I pray she is safe.

Your loving granddaughter,
Erna

P.S. I do not know how much longer they will let me stay here.

❧

A week later Miss Asplund called Erna to her office. When Erna entered, she saw a stranger with a bushy mustache. He stood up and smiled when he saw her, holding out both arms as if to embrace her. His teeth were sharp and white, and he spoke Swedish words mixed with so much English that Erna could barely understand him.

"Your uncle," Miss Asplund said, beaming. "He's come to take you home."

The man spoke affectionately. He held her arm tight. Erna wriggled free. She did not know this man. She did not like his strong vinegary smell.

Miss Asplund frowned. "Erna Anderson, is this

any way to treat a relation who came all the way here to bring you to the rest of your family?"

Erna thought of Alfreda. She had seen her sister bravely curse gentry. She had seen her go boldly where no woman was allowed. Alfreda would not be bullied by this fellow. *Neither will I.* "I have no family here," Erna said. She took a step backward. *I won't be tricked again.*

The stranger bent his face close. Now she could see his cold, dark eyes. They looked as treacherous as the Atlantic at night. "I won't go with you," she said. "You are not my uncle."

Miss Asplund huffed with irritation. "Erna Anderson, you may not get another chance."

"If you are my uncle," Erna said to the stranger, "show me your identification papers." Her voice sounded so forceful, she surprised even herself.

The man's face flushed. He shoved his hands into his pockets. "Why do I need papers? I am your uncle. I can prove it."

"Show the papers then," Erna said.

The man scowled. "I don't have them with me. Little sister, I will go and get them and bring them back."

Erna and Miss Asplund stood in the doorway and watched the man go. "What has gotten into you?" Miss Asplund demanded. "You have just ruined your only chance to make your way in the world."

Erna said nothing. She went back to peeling potatoes and sweeping and hanging blankets on the roof. The man who said he was her uncle never came back.

Weeks passed. Miss Asplund became more ill-humored than ever. "You must go out into the world and find a job," she told Erna. "You cannot stay here forever."

Even though Erna knew that the Immigration Society would never be her home, she did not want to leave. What if Boppa sent a letter? How would he know where she had gone? What if Mama came to America looking for her? She'd never find her.

One day two men appeared at the door. They looked awkward and anxious as they knocked politely. One carried a paper bag. Suspiciously Erna watched the men from the second-story window. She heard Miss Asplund answer the door and lead the men into her office.

Erna tiptoed down the stairs. She lingered in the hallway until Miss Asplund shouted, "Erna Anderson!"

Erna slunk into the office. She did not look at the two men as she sat in a hard chair. Miss Asplund rose and stood beside Erna. She rapped the back of her chair with her sharp knuckle. "This gentleman," she said in a bright voice, "says he is your father. And this is your uncle."

Erna did not say anything.

Miss Asplund leaned over and hissed into Erna's ear, "Use good manners!"

Reluctantly Erna looked up. The taller man who carried the paper bag had a wrinkled, tanned face and gray, thinning hair. He had a tired, sad mouth and blue eyes. The other man, who spoke better Swedish, looked much like the first—only he was shorter and thinner. Both wore American clothes and spoke with a strong American accent.

"Erna," the taller man said. "Do you remember me?"

Erna shook her head. *I will not be tricked.* "Who are you?" she demanded.

"Be polite, girl!" Miss Asplund barked.

The taller man sighed. "I am your father," he said. "And this is your uncle Fred."

Erna felt startled. *How does this stranger know my uncle's name?*

The man called Fred bobbed his head slightly but did not remove his battered hat. He continued to chew something that made an unpleasant bulge in his face.

Erna crossed her arms in front of herself and eyed the two men. Her expression was wary and somber.

"I brought you a present. A banana," the taller man said. He took something long and yellow from the bag. He handed it to Erna. She turned the smooth, hard banana over and over in her hands. She had never seen anything like it in her life. "Eat it," the man said encouragingly.

Erna nibbled on one end. The banana tasted waxy and terrible.

The man called Fred began to laugh.

Erna's face flushed with anger.

"You must peel it first," the taller man said gently. He, too, looked embarrassed.

"I don't want it," Erna said. She handed the banana back. *Why are they making fun of me?*

Self-consciously, the taller man coughed. He slipped the banana back into the bag. "I brought you a jelly doughnut, too," he said. He handed her something round and brown.

Erna sniffed the unfamiliar thing called *jelly doughnut*. It smelled sweet. When she bit into it, there was no hard, waxy peel. Something red squirted out. She stared, horrified as the red, sticky substance crawled down the front of her dress.

The taller man said something that was English—something she couldn't understand. He handed her his handkerchief. In one skittish movement, she thrust the thing called *jelly doughnut* back into his hands. She waved his handkerchief away. She did not like these gifts. She did not like these men. They were trying to make her look foolish. "Go away," she told them and stood to leave.

"Come back here, young lady," Miss Asplund said angrily. "You are bold and sassy."

"It's all right," the taller man said. "She reminds me of her mother. Same hair, same eyes, same temper."

Erna paused and looked at him suspiciously. *Alfreda's the one with the temper.* "What else do you *not* know about me?" she demanded in a haughty voice.

"I know that you were born on the day the cows escaped and broke the strongest fence," the taller man said. "It was a weekday morning during potato picking."

Erna had heard something like this before but could not remember if it was told of her or of Karl. "And what else?"

"When you were born, Balk-Emma tied you inside a shawl and weighed you on the steelyard, and you weighed nearly nine pounds."

Erna sucked in her lip. "What else?"

"You were a steady eater, and your grandmother said that meant you would grow to be good-natured, kind, and generous."

Erna cocked her head. "What happened later — when I was more grown?"

"When your mother went haying, she carried you in a bundle and let you sleep under a bush in the meadow. But she always kept wool shears and a knife with you."

"And why was that?"

"For protection against the trolls who might kidnap you," the taller man said and paused. "But the steel did not protect you against the pismires that bit you and gave you a bad rash."

Slowly Erna lowered herself into the chair again. "And what of the farm? What do you know of my grandfather's farm?"

The taller man closed his eyes and spoke as if he were trying to recall a dream. "There is a big field on one side and a little field on the other. A stone wall runs all around. There are worn stone steps at the doorway of the house, and a trellis arches in the garden where my father planted wild grapes. In the big square barn are two doors—"

Erna took a deep breath. She thought of Boppa's sweet-smelling barn. Dark and cool and safe. "And what of the road?" she demanded, knowing this would be hardest question of all. "Who built the road that goes past the farm?"

The taller man opened his eyes. He scratched his chin as if he felt confused. "The road?"

"Yes, the road," Erna said. Triumphantly she folded her arms in front of herself. *Now I've stumped you.*

"Why the road that runs along the ridge was built long ago by *tomtar.*"

Erna gulped. *"Tomtar?"*

"Tomtar cannot stand to be idle. There was a neighbor then, long, long ago, who was made dizzy in the head by the *tomtar* on his farm. They were always demanding work. They plowed and planted and harvested with such energy, his farm was soon the richest in the parish. They were the ones who dug out the road—right through a terrible swamp."

"Go on," Erna said softly.

"Well, one day the poor fellow was nearly driven mad by their constant demands for more work. He lit his pipe. He tried to think of something to keep these industrious *tomtar* busy. His pipe smoke floated away into the air. That's what gave him an idea for an impossible task. He told the *tomtar* to collect his pipe smoke."

The man called Fred chuckled and shifted the wad inside his mouth to the other cheek.

"Legend has it," the taller man continued, "that after seven years, only one lonely *tomte* returned to the farmer. He had managed to collect a little bit of smoke inside the quill of a feather."

Erna remained silent. She felt confused. This was an ending to the story that Boppa never told. *But why does it sound so familiar?*

"Very quaint," Miss Asplund said approvingly. "Your little anecdote brings back many pleasant memories of the Old Country."

"When Erna was just a toddling child," the taller man explained, "she'd crawl up on my knee. She was a bright, jabbering thing. She'd say over and over, 'Tell the *fjäderspinne!*'"

"*Fjäderspinne?*" Miss Asplund asked.

"The feather tale."

Erna took a deep breath. Now at last she understood who first told her this story. "Papa!" she said and ran to him.

He held her tight in his arms. She buried her

face in his smoky shirt, and for the first time in many long, lonely days, she felt safe.

"Why are you crying, little one?" Papa demanded.

She wiped her face with her sleeve. When she looked up, she could see that his eyes were also filled with tears. "I am crying because I am so happy," she said.

Papa smiled. "I am happy, too. You have grown into a fine, brave, strong girl who knows her own mind. And that is good."

A fine, brave, strong girl. Erna smiled at him shyly. No one had ever called her that before. "How did you find me?"

"Your mother wrote to me of what happened — how you and your sister were on the ship that went down," Papa explained. "It took a long time for her letter to reach me. Now your uncle and I are going to take you home. Your mother will soon join us."

"We are going home?" Erna whispered.

"To Chicago," Papa said, "to start a new life."

Erna stepped out the door of the Swedish Immigration Society into the bright, crowded street. She walked between her father and her uncle. Pausing, she let go of Papa's hand, which was rough and hard from so much work. She slipped off her wooden shoes, stood on the pavement, and wiggled her toes—just as she'd promised Alfreda. Through the holes in her stockings she could feel the cool, hard pavement.

"What are you doing?" her uncle asked, grinning.

"Testing the America-streets," she said. "They are not made of gold, are they?"

Papa chuckled and shook his head. "No, they are not made of gold."

"Doesn't matter," Erna said. She slid her feet back into her shoes. Happily she took Papa's hand again. "Let's go home."

Author's Note

Erna and Alfreda Anderson's story is based on real people and real events. By the time the Andersons left Sweden, more than a million Swedes had "gone over" the Atlantic to begin a new life in North America. Nearly one-quarter of all Swedes living beween 1851 and 1930 emigrated. During this time of exodus, nearly every Swede could claim to know someone in America.

During the early part of the twentieth century, Atlantic steamships offered the fastest, least expensive way for emigrants to make the journey to the United States. On April 10, 1912, the *Titanic*—dubbed "unsinkable" by the press—began her maiden voyage from Southampton, England, to New York. The expected arrival date was April 16.

The *Titanic* was the largest liner ever built—882 feet long, 92 feet wide, and 46,328 tons in weight. On Sunday evening, April 14, the ship steamed along at 22 ½ knots—her fastest speed on the voyage. Unfortunately, the *Titanic* was also heading straight into treacherous floating ice. At 11:40 P.M. the ship smashed against an iceberg. The glancing blow cut a 300-foot gash below the waterline toward the bow on the starboard side. The "watertight" compartments quickly filled with water and pulled the ship down. The *Titanic* sank in just three hours.

On board were 2,227 passengers and crew. Only 705 survived in twenty lifeboats—many of which were rowed away half-filled.

The glamour of the *Titanic*'s first-class clientele and the glittering excess of this enormous, luxurious "floating palace" have long obscured the fates of lesser known, though equally remarkable passengers. Erna and Alfreda Anderson, Berta Nilson, Elin Lindell, Nora Hagarty, and Bridget O'Neill were all listed among *Titanic*'s steerage or third-class passengers. Of these, only Erna Anderson and Berta Nilson survived.

Theirs is an untold story.

Approximately 712 men, women, and children traveled in *Titanic*'s steerage or third class. Like Erna and Alfreda Anderson, they came from many countries—the British Isles, Scandinavia, France, Italy, Poland, the Middle East, and the Far East. Many did not speak English. They were full of hope and on their way to America to begin a new life.

When the *Titanic* sank, sixty percent of the total 329 men, women, and children in first class were saved. Only 25 percent of the 710 men, women, and children in steerage managed to survive. In first class eleven women and children drowned; in steerage, 119 women and children lost their lives. By any estimate, the numbers are appalling.

As soon as the *Carpathia* docked in New York, Senate hearings began to determine the causes of the worst maritime disaster in history. However, few steerage passengers were invited to participate. Many steerage passengers—especially those who could not speak English—drifted off to find relatives and work and start their lives over again.

One of the questions that Senator William Alden Smith repeatedly asked witnesses was if they had seen evidence that third-class passengers were denied access to lifeboats. Again and again

Senator Smith was told there was no prejudice against steerage passengers.

Class restraints, however, existed aboard the *Titanic* the same way they did in the rest of society at the time. "But they were more subtle and far more pernicious than mere iron gates," Wyn Craig Wade writes in *The* Titanic: *End of a Dream.* "Undoubtedly, the worst barriers were the ones within the steerage passengers themselves. Years of conditioning as third-class citizens led a great many of them to give up hope as soon as the crisis became evident."

Language and class barriers, poor ship design, lack of help from stewards, and no direct access to lifeboats—all contributed to the tragic loss of human life among third-class passengers.

Somehow Erna Anderson managed to survive—in spite of the odds. Exactly how and why she made it off the sinking ship we may never know for sure. I like to think that perhaps her sister was responsible for saving her life.

$\mathscr{B}ibliography$

PRIMARY SOURCES AND DOCUMENTS

Titanic Historical Society, *Remember the* Titanic (audiotapes of survivor interviews), Vol. 1–3. Ludlow, MA: 7 C's Press, 1974.

U.S. Congress, Senate, *Hearings of a Subcommittee of the Senate Commerce Committee Pursuant to S. Res. 283, to Investigate the Causes Leading to the Wreck of the White Star Liner* 'Titanic,' 62nd Cong., 2d Sess., 1912, S. Doc 726 (#6167), 1163 pp.

SECONDARY SOURCES

Ballard, Robert D. *Exploring the* Titanic. New York: Scholastic, Inc., 1994.

Barton, H. Arnold. *Letters from the Promised Land: Swedes in America, 1840–1914.* Minneapolis: University of Minnesota Press, 1975.

Blecker, Lone Thygesen and Bleckner, George. *Swedish Folktales and Legends.* New York: Pantheon Books, 1993.

British Government Enquiry. *Report on the Loss of the S.S.* Titanic *Presented to Both Houses of Parliament by Command of His Majesty: 1912.* New York: St. Martin's Press, 1998.

Coan, Peter Morton. *Ellis Island Interviews: In Their Own Words.* New York: Facts on File, 1997.

Gardner, Martin, ed. *The Wreck of the* Titanic *Foretold.* Buffalo: N.Y.: Prometheus Books, 1986.

Gracie, Archibald. *The Truth About the* Titanic. Riverside, Conn.: 7 C's Press, 1973.

Hasselmo, Nils, ed. *Perspectives on Swedish Immigration.* Chicago: Swedish Pioneer Historical Society, 1978.

Heyer, Paul. Titanic *Legacy: Disaster as Media Event and Myth.* Westport, Conn.: Praeger, 1995.

Hoffman, William and Grimm, Jack. *Beyond Reach: The Search for the* Titanic. New York: Beaufort Books, Inc., 1982.

Hoflund, Charles J. *Getting Ahead: A Swedish Immigrant's Reminiscences 1834–1887.* Carbondale, Ill: Southern Illinois University Press, 1989.

Janson, Florence E. *The Background of Swedish Immigration 1840–1930*. New York: Arno Press, 1970.

Jessup, Violet. Titanic *Survivor*. Dobbs Ferry, New York: Sheridan House, 1997.

Knaplund, Paul. *Moorings Old and New: Entries in an Immigrant's Log*. Madison, Wisc.: State Historical Society of Wisconsin, 1963.

Ljungmark, Lars. *Swedish Exodus*. Carbondale, Ill.: Southern Illinois University Press, 1979.

Lloyd, L. *Peasant Life in Sweden*. London: Tinsley Brothers, 1870.

Lord, Walter. *The Night Lives On*. New York: William Morrow and Co., 1986.

Lord, Walter. *A Night to Remember*. New York: Bantam Books, 1997.

McGill, Allyson. *The Swedish Americans*. New York: Chelsea House Publishers, 1988.

Miller, Kerby A. *Emigrants and Exiles: Ireland and the Irish Exodus to North America*. New York: Oxford University Press, 1985.

Moberg, Vilhelm. *When I Was a Child*. New York: Alfred Knopf, 1956.

Moberg, Vilhelm. *The Emigrants*. New York: Simon and Schuster, 1951.

O'Donnell, E.E. *The Last Days of the* Titanic, Niwot, Colo.: Roberts Rinehart Publishers, 1997.

Ostergren, Robert C. *A Community Transplanted: Transatlantic Experience of a Swedish Immigrant Settlement in Upper Midwest 1835–1915*. Madison, Wisc.: University of Wisconsin Press, 1988.

Reade, Leslie. *The Ship That Stood Still*. New York: W.W. Norton and Co., 1993.

Wade, Wyn Craig. *The* Titanic: *End of a Dream*. New York: Penguin, 1986.

Winocour, Jack, ed. *The Story of the* Titanic *As Told by Its Survivors*, New York: Dover Publications Inc., 1960.

About the Author

Trained as a journalist, Laurie Lawlor worked for many years as a freelance writer and editor before devoting herself full-time to the creation of children's books. She enjoys many speaking engagements at schools and libraries, and her books have been nominated for many awards. She lives in Evanston, Illinois, with her husband, son, daughter, and two large Labrador retrievers. Her books include the *Addie Across the Prairie* series, the *Heartland* series, *How to Survive Third Grade*, *The Worm Club*, *Gold in the Hills*, and *Little Women* (a movie novelization). Her nonfiction work, *Shadow Catcher: The Life and Work of Edward S. Curtis*, won the Carl Sandburg Award for nonfiction (1995) and the Golden Kite Honor Book Award (1995).

Turn the page for a preview of
the next American Sisters hardcover
Horseback on the Boston Post Road, 1704
by Laurie Lawlor

Available in December!

"Drop anchor and come aboard, Girl," Goodwife Kemble demanded. Long ago she had given up calling either twin anything but Girl.

Hester sighed. Philena fidgeted. "We're busy, Mistress," Hester called back to her. Hester knew if they went inside to talk to Goodwife Kemble, they'd be trapped in the kitchen for hours.

"Not too busy to make fast," Goodwife Kemble replied, her raspy voice rising. "I haven't heard your catechism. Now splice your patience and cruise down along into the galley. Be quick."

Reluctantly, Hester and her sister trudged into the house. The old woman kept the kitchen as neat and trim as the deck of a well-run ship. Although she was nearly fourscore years,

Goodwife Kemble was spry enough to climb out on to the roof to repair shingles or scamper up a ladder to wash the second-floor windows. She said she liked to go aloft, and protested loudly when her daughter ordered her down.

"So, I hear you're going to sea," Goodwife Kemble said. She sat on a bench with a gray shawl wrapped around her thin shoulders. She held the worn head of her cane in her gnarled hands.

Hester shrugged. "Madame Knight said something about a journey. She didn't mention anything about taking us along."

"She's not taking both of you. Just one. You." Goodwife Kemble lifted the tip of her cane and gave Hester a nudge. "That's why I want to hear your catechism. You set sail today."

"Today?" Hester said in amazement.

"Where?" Philena bleated. "Why?"

"My daughter won't say," Goodwife Kemble confessed, then added in a hushed tone, "I warned her she's sailing too close to the wind. But there's no stopping her when she's in this reckless state of mind."

Hester winked at her sister. *Just another of her fancies. Pay her no mind.* "Now, now, Mistress . . ." she began, half-smiling.

"Don't 'mistress' me. I've sounded it out. She's going. And she's taking one of you and Polly with her. Now say your catechism, the both of you," Goodwife Kemble commanded.

Only one of us? Philena gulped. To humor the ancient woman, she and Hester did as they were told.

"Come now and stand still beside each other," Goodwife Kemble said when they were finished.

"Do we have to?" Miserably, Philena twisted her apron. "Madame Knight says—"

"We must watch the shop while she's away," Hester interrupted.

Goodwife Kemble frowned. "My Sarah's too fat and too old to be wandering the countryside rigged on a horse," Goodwife Kemble said. "What if she meets with Indians or bears or wolves? And what if the weather turns owlish? What then? Why must she go in October, with bad weather ahead? She says nothing, but acts sly and says I'll be taken care of handsomely when she returns. How can she think that delivering the personal belongings of Mr. Trowbridge to his family will afford her such a great reward?"

Hester and Philena exchanged secret glances. *Great reward?* They had always considered Mr. Trowbridge a miserly, lonely, crooked-backed man. He had been one of Madame Knight's many boarders. Before he died, he had worked as a scrivener—a job Goodwife Kemble explained to mean a person who worked in a lawyer's office writing on pieces of paper in beautiful penmanship. He passed away one evening two weeks before and had been quickly buried. All that he left behind were some clothing and a mysterious, small trunk that was locked tight. Perhaps Madame Knight was being promised something valuable in Mr. Trowbridge's will.

"Girl!" Goodwife Kemble leaned forward and examined closely each of the twelve-year-old maidservants. "You can't fool me. I raised you, don't forget. I know all your impudent tricks. Now hold still for once."

Reluctantly, Hester and Philena froze. With elbows intertwined they seemed like a set of pale, identical roots found beneath a rotting log or an apple split perfectly in half or the same line of a hymn sung over and over. It was dizzying to look upon them at the same time. The startled eye moved from one to the other and back again as if to ask, "Can this be? Which is which? Who is who?"

Once a week for as long as they could remember, Goodwife Kemble ordered them to say their catechism and then stand beside each other for her inspection. "Stand up straight," she barked. She reached out with her cane and pushed Hester closer to Philena. "Who is tallest?"

"She is," Philena said, not bothering to look up.

"Who is smartest?"

"She is," Philena said. She glanced at her grinning twin sister.

"Who is the prettiest?" Goodwife Kemble demanded.

"She is," Philena mumbled, even though they had been told all their lives that they looked exactly alike.

"Who is the most patient, prudent, and prayerful?"

"She is," Philena said.

"Who is the most dutiful, kind, and loving?"

For a long moment Philena paused. "She is," she said finally. She felt a choking inside her throat. *What if Hester really does leave me behind?*

"God go with you," Goodwife Kemble said and studied Philena closely. She bowed her head and made an extra silent prayer. "Amen."

"But you said I'm not the one who's leaving," Philena protested, her voice quavering.

Goodwife Kemble glared at Philena. "Do not be saucy and impudent with me, Girl! I know exactly *who* you are."

Philena whispered her apology and made a little curtsy. She felt glad when Hester grabbed her arm and pulled her outdoors. But just as they stumbled toward freedom, Madame Knight caught them both by the necks of their dresses and hauled them into the house again like two flounders dangling from a hook.

Before they could protest, they found themselves standing in the middle of the keeping-room.

Goodwife Kemble hobbled in from the kitchen and took a seat in the corner. "Is it true?" Philena asked Madame Knight.

"Goodwife Kemble said—"

"A journey today—"

"But I won't go."

"Can you ever speak without interrupting each other?" Madame Knight demanded. "Your habits are most irritating. She paced before them. I wished to tell you myself," she continued. "Once again my mother has completely disregarded my instructions."

Goodwife Kemble beamed happily. She liked nothing better than a bit of mutiny now and then.

"We leave this afternoon," Madame Knight continued.

This afternoon. Hester and Philena's faces filled with shock. Their mouths hung open in disbelief. *Can it be possible?* The idea of separation stunned them. For several moments they could not think of anything to say. Philena stared at a knothole. Hester studied her dirty feet.

And then Hester began to weep. Of course when she began to weep, so did Philena. Soon they were both wailing louder and louder until Madame Knight put her hands over her ears and had to shut the front door for fear that the neighbors would think she was abusing her servants.

"Enough!" Madame Knight cried. "It is only a

journey. We leave today and we shall return as soon as we can. There is not a moment to lose. We are already late in our departure. I need one of you to stay here to watch the shop and help my mother. I need one of you to go to assist me and Polly. What is more simple to understand than that?"

Neither Hester nor Philena was willing to understand. All that they knew was that their lives would be wrenched apart. The thought was as painful as if they were both about to have an arm torn away.

"I cannot go," Hester choked between sobs. "I cannot."

"Do not make her," Philena protested. "She is all that I have in the world."

"You thankless wights!" Madame Knight declared. "I took you in out of the goodness of my heart. I raised you. When the Boston authorities brought you to me, scrawny as a pair of stray cats, I said I'd feed you and dress you and house you. Bring you up as proper Christians. For what? A few miserable shillings a year they give me. You *owe* me your time. You owe me far more than just that. You owe me your lives."

Hester and Philena shivered as if the room had suddenly become very cold.

"You will do as I say," Madame Knight said, "or you will find yourselves in worse circumstances. Your time can be disposed of easily enough. I could send one of you to Virginia. Do not cross me on this." Her gray eyes looked hard. Her mouth's expression was stony.

Philena rubbed her face with her dirty sleeve. Hester sniffed loudly. They had heard this threat countless times. They knew they still had nine years left on their indentured contract. In nine years they would reach their majority—age twenty-one—and they would be free. Until then, Madame Knight could split them apart anytime she wished and sell their remaining time to anyone who wanted to buy a servant's services. And the very worst place for a servant was Virginia. Some rumors said it was the hard labor and the beatings. Others claimed it was the heat and the disease. Whatever the reason, servants sent to Virginia plantations were never heard from again.

"Come now, Girl," Goodwife Kemble said gently to sniffling Hester and Philena. "You'll simply keep your weather eye peeled and you'll be reunited when spring comes again. That's not so far off. Why don't you both go above deck for some fresh air? You're going to make yourself pretty nigh fin out if you keep up your blubbering."

Gratefully, Hester and Philena stumbled out the back door. They walked down the path to the rail fence that separated Madame Knight's property from the common pasture. "You could pretend you were ill and unable to travel," Philena suggested.

"She'd simply take you instead." Hester cocked her head. Beyond the pasture they heard the *clank-clank-clank* of the blacksmith shoeing horses. *For the journey.*

Hester blew her nose loudly. "And I suppose you know why Madame Knight chose me for the journey?"

"Because you are the tallest, prettiest, smartest, most kind, dutiful, and loving?"

Hester made a face and shook her head. She felt surprised by how wretchedly stupid her sister could be sometimes. "She picked me to go with her to keep me out of trouble—far from home and far away from the shop. She left the good twin behind. I've heard her tell Goodwife Kemble that you're the one who never vexes or contradicts. She trusts you."

"You confess your faults too easily, Hester-Phina," Philena replied.

Hester smiled at the sound of their special name. It seemed a kind of comfort. She watched Philena sit on a stump and pick a scraggly sprig of wayward mint. She twirled it between her callused fingers. The sharp green smell reminded Philena of biting salt spray along the ocean when they went to gather clams. By the time Hester returned, it might be spring again. Spring seemed like a long way away.

"Don't look so sad. Now you're making me

miserable, too," Hester said and frowned. "What choice do we have? None. You know that. I must go. And soon I'll return and everything will be just the way it was before I left. I promise. You will be fine. I will be fine, too," she said in a bright voice.

But they both knew she wasn't telling the truth.

"Girls, that's enough lying about lag-last, shiftless, and useless," Madame Knight bellowed from the doorway. She gathered her long skirt to keep it from the mud and hurried out of the house. Over one plump arm she carried a basket filled with gifts from their neighbors. Jams and jellies and fresh bread wrapped in clean cloth. "There is work to be done. And Polly? Where is she? We will never be ready to leave at this rate."

"Haven't seen her, Mistress," Hester replied. Madame Knight's only daughter was the apple of her eye. Over the years Hester and her sister had learned that it was safest not to speak when Polly's name was mentioned. Saying anything almost always landed them in trouble.

"Come here and take this," Madame Knight said. When the girls came closer, Philena took the basket from her. "Which one are you? Doesn't matter. See what you can fit into the tuck-a-muck. And don't forget the box of food when it's time to leave. We shall be lucky to find decent provisions not outrageously priced at inns along the Post Road."

While Philena disappeared into the kitchen,

Hester followed Madame Knight to the barn. "Mistress, can you tell me where we're going?" Hester asked.

"No, I cannot," Madame Knight replied. "I have been told not to reveal our destination."

Mr. Trowbridge's relatives are certainly a suspicious lot! Hester decided to rethink her strategy. "What route shall we travel?" she asked innocently.

"We will ride south along the Post Road," Madame Knight said, "toward New York."

"We are going to New York?" Hester asked. She felt sick to her stomach. She had only ridden half a dozen times in her life. "Is that not very far?"

"I did not say we are going to New York, Girl. I said we are riding in that direction."

Suddenly, Hester felt confused and disheartened. *Doesn't she know exactly where she's going?* She looked into the eyes of her mistress's horse and did not feel the least bit of confidence. The villainously ugly creature had a crazy, wild glare. The other two horses were so abnormally broad-backed that riding them would be like sitting on a table with her feet hanging over the side, resting on the sidesaddle's double stirrups. She and Polly would practically need ladders to climb atop their backs. Even so, there was always the possibility of falling off or being knocked to the ground. *This journey is headed toward disaster.* "Mistress, why can you not—"

"You know the old saying," Madame Knight

warned, " 'Curiosity killed the cat.' I suggest you ask no more questions."

"Mama?" Polly cried. She scurried around the barn. The whites of her large gray eyes were red. Her pale face was streaked with tears. "I cannot go with so few dresses. What will people think when they see me wearing the same dress over and over again? I will be humiliated."

Madame Knight took a deep breath. She put her dimpled fists on her broad hips and looked at her pretty, wailing daughter. "We have no choice, my dear. There is not space."

"I won't go then," Polly announced.

Hester breathed a great sigh of relief. She would be glad to make this ill-fated trip without the bothersome, spoiled creature.

"We have already discussed this," Madame Knight replied mysteriously. "This is your opportunity to meet quality people. You have never been outside of Boston. Now, my dear, please dry your eyes and finish packing your clothing. I am sure that we will find plenty of fine dressmakers in New Haven."

New Haven! Hester scowled. They were going all the way to New Haven for a new wardrobe for Polly?

Madame Knight's comment seemed to make perfect sense to her daughter. With revived spirits, Polly shoved her way past Hester. "Out of my way,

"Girl," she snarled and marched back to the house. Hester could not retaliate. Not with Madame Knight watching. *Just wait*, she thought.

It was nearly three o'clock before the horses were saddled and Mr. Trowbridge's belongings were fastened with ropes behind Madame Knight's saddle. She and Polly and Hester said their final, tearful farewells before setting off behind fat Captain Luist, who promised to accompany them as far as the first town on the Post Road. A small group of neighbors and friends followed the horseback riders to the place where Moon Street forked. "Good-bye! Good-bye!" they shouted.

Philena stood outside the shop and waved a handkerchief and sobbed as if her heart would break. She could not believe that Hester was really leaving. As she watched her sister ride away, she felt a terrible wrenching emptiness that throbbed like a toothache. *What will I do without Hester?*

Hester took one look back at her sister standing in the muddy street. Hester blinked hard and tried to appear brave as the sidesaddle rocked dangerously from side to side. *Indians. Cold wind. Deep snow. Bears and wolves.*

As she moved farther and farther away from Philena, she felt as if she were watching herself becoming smaller and smaller. A memory returned. Hester recalled when she was a little girl and glanced for the first time into Madame Knight's looking glass. She thought she was seeing her sister smile and reach out to her. She even tried to lift and look behind the looking glass, certain that Hester-Phina must be hiding there. When she discovered her sister had vanished, Hester burst into tears and cried inconsolably.

That was how she felt at this very moment: abandoned and alone.

Look for the next American Sisters title
Horseback on the Boston Post Road, 1704
by Laurie Lawlor
Available from Minstrel® Books